SAFE SKIPPER

A PRACTICAL GUIDE TO MANAGING RISK AT SEA

Simon Jollands & Rupert Holmes

ADLARD COLES NAUTICAL

BLOOMSBURY

LONDON • NEW DELHI • NEW YORK • SYDNEY

Adlard Coles Nautical
An imprint of Bloomsbury Publishing Plc

50 Bedford Square, London, WC1B 3DP, UK
1385 Broadway, New York, NY 10018, USA

www.bloomsbury.com

Adlard Coles, Adlard Coles Nautical and the Buoy logo are
trademarks of Bloomsbury Publishing Plc

First published 2015

British Library Cataloguing-in-Publication Data
A catalogue record for this book is available from the British
Library.

ISBN:	PB:	978-1-4729-0914-5
	ePDF:	978-1-4729-1548-1
	ePub:	978-1-4729-1547-4

10 9 8 7 6 5 4 3 2 1

Designer: Stuart Batley
Typeset in Arial and Gill Sans
Printed and bound in China by Toppan Leefung

To find out more about our authors and books visit
www.bloomsbury.com. Here you will find extracts, author
interviews, details of forthcoming events and the option to sign
up for our newsletters.

Cover photographs (clockwise from top left)
© Shutterstock © Rick Tomlinson Photography © Kass Schmitt
© Simon Jollands © Shutterstock © Patrick Roach Picture Agency

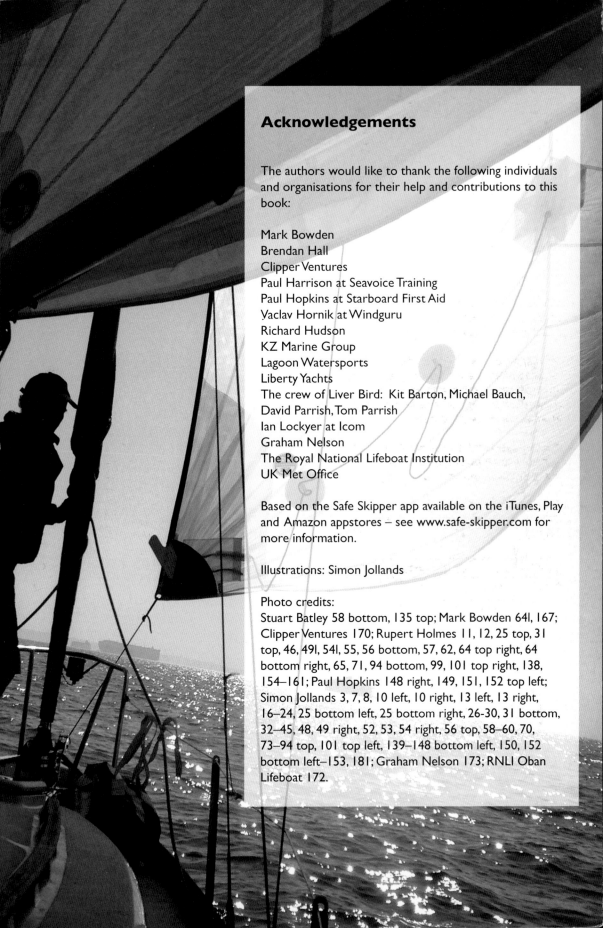

Acknowledgements

The authors would like to thank the following individuals and organisations for their help and contributions to this book:

Mark Bowden
Brendan Hall
Clipper Ventures
Paul Harrison at Seavoice Training
Paul Hopkins at Starboard First Aid
Vaclav Hornik at Windguru
Richard Hudson
KZ Marine Group
Lagoon Watersports
Liberty Yachts
The crew of Liver Bird: Kit Barton, Michael Bauch, David Parrish, Tom Parrish
Ian Lockyer at Icom
Graham Nelson
The Royal National Lifeboat Institution
UK Met Office

Based on the Safe Skipper app available on the iTunes, Play and Amazon appstores – see www.safe-skipper.com for more information.

Illustrations: Simon Jollands

Photo credits:
Stuart Batley 58 bottom, 135 top; Mark Bowden 64l, 167; Clipper Ventures 170; Rupert Holmes 11, 12, 25 top, 31 top, 46, 49l, 54l, 55, 56 bottom, 57, 62, 64 top right, 64 bottom right, 65, 71, 94 bottom, 99, 101 top right, 138, 154–161; Paul Hopkins 148 right, 149, 151, 152 top left; Simon Jollands 3, 7, 8, 10 left, 10 right, 13 left, 13 right, 16–24, 25 bottom left, 25 bottom right, 26-30, 31 bottom, 32–45, 48, 49 right, 52, 53, 54 right, 56 top, 58–60, 70, 73–94 top, 101 top left, 139–148 bottom left, 150, 152 bottom left–153, 181; Graham Nelson 173; RNLI Oban Lifeboat 172.

CONTENTS

Introduction

We enjoy ourselves on the water knowing full well there are risks attached. The same applies to most sporting activities and many leisure pursuits, but this does not put us off indulging in such fulfilling pastimes. Whether we are going afloat for a few hours, a few days, a few weeks or longer, skippers of recreational vessels should always consider the margins of safety and ensure we are working within them. Good seamanship is an art that takes time to master. It calls for a combination of knowledge, experience, awareness, instinct and good working practices which are built up over a period of time, backed up with intensive training both ashore and afloat.

This book is not intended as a short cut that avoids the tried and tested processes that lead to good seamanship. Instead, we hope through identifying some of the key skills entailed, both novice and experienced skippers will find the content helpful and a useful reference for brushing up their knowledge, reducing risks when going afloat, ensuring the safety of crew and vessel comes first, being prepared for unexpected problems and for reminders of how to deal with them if they occur.

What is the secret of becoming a safe skipper? Partly this comes down to the mental attitude of the person responsible for their vessel and crew – a calm, confident personality who does not shout at their crew, reassures the inexperienced, anticipates problems and avoids unnecessary risks. All are great attributes but count for little if the fundamental skills of seamanship are lacking. Perhaps above all a safe skipper is someone who never underestimates the sea.

PREPARATION
Principles of seaworthiness and seamanship

Safety at sea is not as simple as just spending money adding shiny new emergency equipment such as liferafts, dan buoys, distress flares, EPIRBs and so on.

While these items are of course important, it's better to view them as an insurance that offers a potential lifeline when things have already gone badly wrong. They are, in effect, the nautical equivalent of the airbags in your car: very reassuring to have, but nevertheless items you will not need to activate.

More than anything else, what keeps us safe at sea is our attitude to risk. Given that it's impossible to eliminate risk, we have to be continuously alive to the constantly changing situations that are an inevitable part of going to sea, analysing them for dangers so that any current or future risks can be identified. It's then possible to build into your plans ways to mitigate these risks, along with a margin of safety that's appropriate to the prevailing conditions.

So what are the biggest potential dangers you're likely to encounter? Fortunately, the list is surprisingly short. For individual crew members the key hazards are:

1. Fatigue, seasickness and hypothermia
2. Sunburn and sunstroke
3. Accidents involving dinghies and tenders
4. Head injuries from the boom or mainsheet
5. Falling overboard
6. Crushing fingers in a winch

The biggest dangers to the boat itself that may lead to serious incidents are as follows:

1. Bumping into solid objects such as land, rocks or other vessels
2. Failure of key equipment
3. Severe weather
4. Fire
5. Sinking

Given the potential dangers of the sea, both lists are surprisingly short. Of course, there are other things that may go wrong, but most other crisis situations you might encounter, while potentially frightening at the time, are less likely to be life-threatening or result in serious injury.

Cascade of events

When serious incidents at sea are analysed, one factor always stands out: very few have a single cause. Instead, most are the result of a chain of events with a catastrophic conclusion. In many cases, it would only require any one of the many links in the chain to be broken to stop the situation cascading into an ever more serious state.

The most important lesson to draw from this is that, when faced with a potential emergency situation, it must be tackled in a calm and logical fashion. That may sound obvious and straightforward, but when things start to go wrong the reality is that it will require a sustained and conscious effort to avoid running around in an adrenaline-fuelled panic that can easily make things worse.

Rather than attempting to make instant life or death decisions when the pressure is on, it's easier to remember drills and routines – that's why man overboard drill practice is so important. Equally, for an inexperienced crew, frequent practice at reefing is also beneficial, and the same holds true for anchoring. The more these and other activities are routine, the easier it is to carry them out under pressure, without creating new problems.

Avoiding personal dangers

1 Fatigue, seasickness and hypothermia

Fatigue, seasickness and hypothermia may be encountered individually, but also can frequently occur together, often with each element helping to feed the others. Each can be debilitating on their own, impairing decision-making ability and eliminating any enthusiasm for deck work. When all three occur together it's a potent combination that can sap resolve too and is a common element in a number of rescues of yacht crews.

Fatigue is easily avoided through getting enough sleep before sailing and through taking ample periods of time off watch on a longer passage. It's also important to have adequate hydration and nutrition, both of which are all too frequently neglected when under way. The latter is doubly important for those who normally live a sedate desk-bound life – on a yacht, by mid afternoon

▼ *Any crew member can suffer from seasickness, however fit and healthy. The sufferer here was working at the chart table below in a heavy swell, which brought on the sickness.*

°C	Wind chill temperatures Windspeed (knots)							
	5	10	15	20	25	30	35	40
20	19.0	16.1	15.1	14.5	13.4	12.6	12.0	12.4
18	16.8	14.1	12.4	11.2	10.4	9.8	9.4	9.2
16	14.7	11.6	9.8	8.3	7.4	6.7	6.3	6.0
14	12.5	9.1	6.9	5.4	4.4	3.7	3.2	2.9
12	10.4	6.5	4.2	2.5	1.4	0.6	0.0	-0.3
10	8.2	4.0	1.4	-0.4	-1.6	-2.5	-3.1	-3.5
8	6.1	1.5	-1.3	-3.3	-4.7	-5.6	-6.3	-6.7
6	3.9	-1.0	-4.1	-6.2	-7.7	-8.7	-9.4	-9.8
4	1.8	-3.5	-6.8	-9.1	-10.7	-11.8	-12.5	-13.0
2	-0.4	-6.1	-9.6	-12.0	-13.7	-14.9	-15.7	-16.2
0	-2.5	-8.6	-12.3	-14.9	-16.7	-18.0	-18.8	-19.4
-2	-4.7	-11.1	-15.1	-17.8	-19.7	-21.1	-22.0	-22.5
-4	-6.8	-13.6	-17.8	-20.7	-22.7	-24.1	-25.1	-25.7
-6	-9.0	-16.1	-20.6	-23.6	-25.7	-27.2	-28.3	-28.9
-8	-11.1	-18.7	-23.3	-26.5	-28.8	-30.3	-31.4	-32.1
-10	-13.3	-21.2	-26.1	-29.4	-31.8	-33.4	-34.5	-35.2

▲ *Wind increases the rate that a body loses heat, because as wind blows over the skin it evaporates moisture, causing a cooling effect. Different people feel wind chill in different ways, depending on body size and mass. This chart provides a useful guide, eg 20 knots of wind at 10°C will feel close to freezing. Humidity and pressure also affect wind chill.*

you may already have used as many calories as during the whole of a normal day, which can result in low blood sugar unless you're eating more than usual.

▼ *The boom is a lethal weapon. Make sure the crew are aware and guard against accidental gybes.*

2 Sunburn and sunstroke

It always feels colder afloat than onshore so sunburn and sunstroke are easily underestimated, yet just as when skiing, there's also more glare and reflection on the water than on land. You therefore need to take the risks seriously, use sunscreen, remain well hydrated and watch out for potential problems among fellow crew – it's much easier to see the initial signs in someone else than to self-diagnose.

3 Dinghies and tenders

The dangers inherent in using a dinghy to get ashore from a mooring or anchorage are all too easily underestimated, often by a wide margin. However, many more sailors are lost from their tenders, or when transferring between dinghy and yacht, than are lost at sea.

Lifejackets should be worn in a dinghy and you also need a bullet-proof means of signalling distress in the event of problems. When getting in and out of the dinghy, tie it to the yacht or dock with both bow and stern lines – this will prevent the dinghy swinging away from the yacht, which is the most common reason for people falling between the two.

As always, try to predict changing conditions. An apparently benign trip ashore on a sunny evening may turn into a completely different situation if the wind is forecast to strengthen and the tide will be ebbing fast when you return to the boat.

4 Head injuries from the boom or mainsheet

A head injury from a gybe is potentially the most serious danger of all, and capable of causing a fatality. It's important that everyone on board is aware of the danger, especially the hazard zone for boats with cockpit-mounted mainsheet systems. As well as pointing this out in initial briefings, the skipper must also ensure everyone's safety is assured during a planned gybe.

However, it's accidental gybes that lead to the majority of incidents. Given that by definition an accidental gybe is an unplanned event, at first sight it might appear difficult to guard against this danger. However, it's possible to ensure that accidental gybes never happen. While on a raceboat with a very experienced, well drilled and fully focused team on board I might be happy to run dead downwind with full sail set in 25 knots of wind, I'd take a very different approach on a cruising boat with a less talented and alert crew.

As a Yachtmaster Instructor, for instance, if the apparent wind was aft of the beam I would, without fail, take one of three courses of action to ensure there could never be an accidental

gybe. If it was for a relatively short time I might sit near the helm, so that I could coach the driver to nudge the boat in the right direction, or even take over myself if necessary. Alternatively a preventer would be used to stop the boom coming across in the event of the wind getting on the wrong side of the sail. The third option is to eliminate the problem by dropping the mainsail.

5 Falling overboard

Falling overboard has the potential to be one of the most frightening and life-threatening experiences that can be encountered at sea. The old cliché that prevention is better than cure is particularly apt for MOB situations and it's crucial to give thought to making certain everyone stays on board. Harness-wearing discipline is vital and crew members should be encouraged to build up a constant awareness of potential dangers, as well as looking out for other people, especially those who are less experienced. If the worst happens, wearing a properly fitted lifejacket with a crotch strap can multiply survival times 10–15 fold, especially if it's fitted with a spray hood and light.

6 Crushing fingers in a winch

The loads encountered on modern yachts are all too easily underestimated. For instance, the genoa sheets of a 35-foot cruising boat may carry well in excess of half a tonne – a level that must be handled with care. Therefore all crew members should be briefed in good line-handling discipline, including how to add and remove turns from the winch drum, how to safely ease or release the sheet and so on. Anchor windlasses need to be treated with similar respect.

▼ Fingers and thumbs can easily be caught in a winch if it is not used correctly, both when grinding and releasing a sheet under load. Ensure all crew know the drill.

Biggest dangers a yacht may encounter

1 Collision with solid objects such as land, rocks or other vessels

Solid objects such as land, rocks or other vessels are external dangers that need to be identified long before there's any risk of them becoming a real problem. The first stage is to identify dangers such as busy shipping channels or shoal areas as part of your pre-planning, while the second is ensuring you don't fall foul of them when under way. The latter is easier if your plan avoids fixed dangers; and, if shipping is operating in restricted waters, that you know where you can safely go to keep clear of them and what their likely routes are.

This should be straightforward in good visibility, but may not be so easy at night or in restricted visibility. It doesn't take full-on fog to prevent you seeing a ship until it's within a couple of miles. With a closing speed of 20 knots, for example, that gives just six minutes to assess risk of collision and take avoiding action.

2 Failure of key equipment

There are plenty of examples of yachts that have overcome significant difficulties such as broken masts and rudders and have reached harbour using their own resources. However, equipment failure also has the potential to be incredibly demoralising and has caused a good number of crews to lose confidence in their vessel, leading to unnecessary abandonments.

▲ *Pre-planning will reduce the risk of running aground. If the worst happens, knowing how to quickly assess the situation and take swift action is essential.*

▼ *Regular checks of key equipment above and below deck will enable problems to be solved before they occur.*

The first step to avoiding problems in this respect is daily checks of the engine, rig and other equipment. This procedure will identify many imminent failures in advance and will also help you to get to know your boat better and improve your understanding of its various systems.

If you do encounter gear failure, there are a couple of key questions that will guide your next steps:

> **Pre-start, check:**
> - Is it an item that offers convenience such as ease of handling, and therefore isn't absolutely essential, or is it one that's vital to the operation of the boat?
> - If the latter, can the broken item be readily substituted or replaced?

It is worth noting the large number of sailing yachts that are rescued by lifeboat following engine failure. The lack of a working engine often seems to cause skipper and crew to lose more confidence in the vessel than is logical. As well as the basic daily checks, make sure your engine is serviced up to date and in good order. You also need to know how to carry out basic repairs including diagnosing starting problems, changing fuel filters, bleeding air out of the fuel system and replacing the water pump impeller. A short marine engine maintenance course is a worthwhile investment of time and money.

▼ Daily checks of engine oil and cooling systems may delay departure by a few minutes but will help prevent engine failure at sea.

 **TIPS**

Stay in command

When things start to go wrong, your crew will be looking to you for reassurance that you are taking positive steps that will keep the situation under some kind of control. However, it's worth noting that strong leadership doesn't prevent you using the skills and experience of others on board to help figure out solutions – in many cases crew members will have specialist skills or knowledge that may enable them to figure out viable solutions even if they don't have extensive boating experience.

In challenging situations I like to explain to crew members why things have gone wrong, what the new plan is, and what the new plan B is in case that goes wrong. It can also be very reassuring for crew members if you identify what you consider to be the likely worst-case scenario and your initial plan to deal with that should it happen.

This kind of approach will demonstrate that you have the situation under control and are in control of the overall situation and simultaneously helps people to regain an appreciation of the intrinsic resilience of the boat.

▼ Keeping a good lookout all around you is imperative at all times, whatever the visibility. A ship approaching fast from astern makes hardly any sound and can catch out an unwary crew.

3 Severe weather

Many sailors would put this further up the list, but while severe weather is certainly an important factor and not to be underestimated, most rescues at sea are carried out in more benign conditions. Even in challenging circumstances, a key effect of a strong wind is to uncover existing deficiencies in the boat, rather than the vessel simply being overwhelmed by the force of the wind.

The loads in the rig, for instance, reach a maximum when the boat is fully powered up – often in no more than a force 3 when sailing to windward. On the other hand, a rough day is exactly when any debris that might otherwise reside undisturbed on the bottom of the fuel tank will get stirred up and be likely to block filters. Equally, the consequences of encountering unforeseen problems in bad weather can be significant. In addition, fatigue, seasickness and cold can all play a much larger part in the equation than on a fine day.

What constitutes bad weather will vary considerably depending on your experience, the design of your boat and the equipment carried. Those with lots of experience of sailing in a force 7 and even occasional gales will clearly cope more easily than a crew that has never previously encountered more than a force 5. Similarly, a boat with well-cut heavy weather and storm sails will be able to make ground to windward and away from a lee shore long after one that relies on an old and stretched deeply reefed roller genoa in such conditions.

4 Fire

Almost everything a modern boat is made of is highly combustible, so a fire on board is potentially one of the most frightening incidents that can happen at sea. A decent-sized fire extinguisher can be extremely effective, providing it's used promptly, as is a fire blanket for dealing with cooking fires.

However, this is another instance in which prevention is the route to peace of mind. That means having a first-rate gas system that's properly maintained, including periodic replacement of flexible pipes and regulators. It also means that petrol for outboard engines should be stowed on deck, allowing the vapour from any spillages to escape, rather than stowing the fuel in a cockpit locker, where it may leak into the bilge.

It's equally important to keep the electrical system well maintained, with the batteries firmly secured in place – a short circuit in a 12V system is capable of starting an electrical fire.

5 Sinking

Fortunately, sinking is a surprisingly rare occurrence with modern yachts and is usually

the result of external factors such as grounding, hitting debris such as a container, or collision with another vessel. However, there has also been a small number of instances in which skin fittings have succumbed to extensive electrolytic action, or the speed log transducer has been damaged, resulting in leaks developing.

In addition to pipework being double-clipped to skin fittings, a tapered softwood plug of the correct size should be tied to the fitting to prevent it floating away and becoming lost in the event of the boat being flooded. For the same reason, bilge pump handles should be secured by a lanyard.

When a yacht starts to fill with water it's easy to get a false perspective – when the boat is heeled it takes surprisingly little before it starts to wash over the lee bunk in the saloon – and many boats have been abandoned prematurely for this reason. On the other hand, if you really do have a serious problem – and it's clear the boat really is sinking rapidly – then you need to take action to raise the alarm and abandon ship immediately.

▼ *Severe weather is a great test for crew and boat. A skipper should know how to deal with storm conditions and be prepared well in advance as the storm approaches, ensuring storm sails are ready, crew are clipped on and the boat is ready to deal with the conditions.*

Local v long-distance cruising

The degree of preparation, knowledge and equipment needed will vary considerably, depending on the type of sailing you have planned. Fine summer afternoons pottering around sheltered waters are naturally much less onerous than crossing the English Channel, or a voyage from Portugal to the Canary Islands.

However, at a basic level there's still much common ground, relating, for example, to the fact that (almost all) keelboats can sink, that a yacht may be knocked down by a breaking wave even when close to shore, and that if heavy items such as tools, batteries, ground tackle and tins of food are allowed to move around they can damage either the vessel or crew members. Similarly, losing a washboard in heavy weather could spell disaster, so attaching them to the boat with a lanyard makes sense, and the companionway should be capable of being secured from above and below deck. Anyone who doubts the need for this should remember that the overfalls that form off many prominent headlands have the potential for breaking waves that will lay a capable vessel on her beam ends.

A boat undertaking longer voyages will also need to be equipped to be self sufficient, potentially for long periods of time, with the spares and tools to undertake significant maintenance when necessary. It will also need a higher level of equipment – including first-rate ground tackle that will hold in a gale, plus heavy weather and storm sails.

▲ *Headlands such as Start Point, Devon, UK have well-charted overfalls. By staying well offshore, breaking waves can be avoided and the boat remains safe.*

At least two bilge pumps are needed, including one that can be operated from below and a second that can be operated on deck, with all cockpit lockers closed. An emergency tiller should also be provided in case the regular one breaks (easily done if someone falls against it in heavy weather) or the wheel steering system fails. In both cases, make sure you know how they are fitted – this is not something you want to be trying to figure out on a black night two miles off a lee shore in a rising gale.

▼ *It is important to keep the crew properly nourished and not skip meals. Avoid alcohol and ensure no one gets dehydrated.*

Total rudder loss is also something that must be prepared for in advance. Offshore racing regulations, for instance, require crews to have rehearsed at least one method of steering their boat without the rudder and cruisers ought to follow suit.

Many of the hard-won lessons of the ill-fated 1979 Fastnet Race are just as applicable today, as is this profound advice from the official inquiry report into the race: 'In the 1979 race the sea showed that it can be a deadly enemy and that those who go to sea for pleasure must do so in full knowledge that they may encounter danger of the highest order.'

Although both weather forecasting and the boats we sail have improved enormously in the past few decades, it would be complacent to assume that a storm of equal intensity could not ravage a yacht on a passage of more than two or three days.

▼ *Is all this gear really necessary? For local cruising probably not, but there is nothing excessive here for long-distance cruising, with self-steering, solar panels and safety gear much in evidence.*

TIPS

The human factor

Whether on an afternoon's sail that turns into an unexpected upwind slog, a 60-mile crossing of the English Channel, or a five-day crossing of the Bay of Biscay, there's arguably more chance of the skipper and crew being the weak link in the chain than problems with the boat.

You need to carefully pace yourself physically to keep functioning, with adequate food, drink and rest. In particular it's worth remembering that sleep deprivation quickly leads to severely impaired capacity for flexible and innovative thinking, exaggerates tendencies to take risks, and reduces motivation.

Equally, we are not able to function effectively for long periods of time without proper nutrition – even on day sails it's worth having a plan to feed everyone on board, plus further additional supplies in case the passage takes longer than expected.

Margins of safety

'How safe is safe enough?' is a question, often rhetorical, that can all too often appear to have no tangible answers. However, it's not too difficult to lay down ground rules that provide useful guidelines.

Given a light offshore wind, good visibility and a rising tide in an area you know well, it may be perfectly acceptable to skirt less than one or two hundred metres from the edge of a well-defined and well-marked sandbank.

Providing the boat is not travelling at speed, the danger is small and you can expect to have a number of cues to guide your progress. This means, as long as you are alert to those cues, you can take appropriate action should any of them warn you of something being not quite right.

However, the same sandbank in an onshore wind gusting 30 knots and a falling tide may demand a safety margin of several miles. In these conditions, as well as ensuring you miss both the sand and any disturbed water around it, you also need a

▼ *In deteriorating visibility, it is wise to keep plenty of distance between you and the land, allowing a good margin of safety should conditions worsen and navigation becomes more challenging.*

buffer in case something goes wrong. If a jib sheet parts, for instance, and you only have a couple of minutes before the boat is pushed on to the sand, you will be in a perilous situation. However, if you have 20 minutes in which to replace the line, or retrieve it from the water to ensure it's completely clear of the prop before starting the engine, you can be confident of having ample time – and of being able to deal with the unlikely event of a further problem. Equally, in areas that you know less well, you will want to leave larger safety margins – even with the best of modern electronics your navigation may not be spot on, especially if strong tides are prevalent.

Similar principles apply for passing other vessels. While as a sailing boat in open water you can expect a ship to alter course or speed to give way, as stated in the Colregs Rule 18: Responsibilities between vessels – there comes a point at which you effectively pass control of the situation to the other vessel. Given the consequences of it going wrong, there's a strong argument for avoiding the close-quarters situation in the first place. If doing so, make sure you make your intentions clear at an early stage so that you don't confuse a give-way vessel that is preparing to take avoiding action, as stated in Colregs Rule 17: Action by stand-on vessels – see pages 52–53.

▼ *These two boats are in open water and will pass very close. The catamaran on port tack is the give-way vessel.*

TIPS

Time pressure

This may sound innocuous – many of us lead a life onshore that's shaped to a large degree by schedules – but time pressure at sea can easily lead to the kind of situations you would prefer not to encounter.

It might simply be setting sail on a Sunday afternoon, in a little more wind than forecast, in order to get home in good time for work on Monday morning. In many cases this may be a good thing, in that it forces you to push your boundaries and gain experience that you otherwise might shy away from. However, if pushed beyond sensible limits it also has the potential to go badly wrong.

If an incident of any kind develops, you have a double-whammy because you will be slowed further, which will add yet more pressure to the situation. It's easy to see how a problem can then appear to get out of hand, even if it's one that you might have happily coped with in other circumstances.

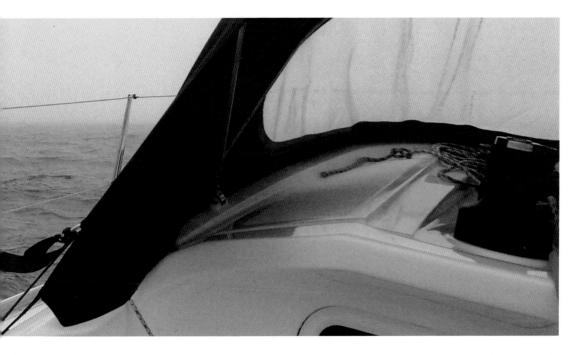

Vessel checks: hull, rigging, ground tackle, engine, seacocks, gas system, electrical system

All vessels and equipment need inspecting on a regular basis. If in doubt when inspections and servicing should be done for your vessel, a good place to start is to read instruction manuals, contact manufacturers and to consult your surveyor. Then make up a plan to ensure you keep up to date with the work that needs carrying out. Keep a record of your boat's history and if it has had several owners, get in contact with them to find out when equipment was replaced and serviced in the past. You might also be able to access old surveys if you don't already have them. While manuals may not be as entertaining as boating magazines or online forums, the information will be specific to your equipment and vessel.

There is plenty to think about. Many experienced skippers make a number of checklists to suit their vessel, to help ensure no jobs are forgotten when the boat is ashore over the winter and before each trip.

Hull
When the boat is out of the water, do visual inspections of the hull to check for distortion and hull damage. Keel joints and bolts need to be checked especially carefully; if in any doubt, ask a specialist to look at the keel. Keel bands on motor boats need a close check to ensure there is no wear in the fastenings.

Different hull materials have their own strengths and weaknesses, with particular things to look out for. For example, composite hulls need to be checked for scratches and chips in the gelcoat, impact cracks and osmosis. Aluminium and steel hulls need checking for signs of corrosion and electrolytic pitting in the plating. Wooden hulls need checking for splits in the timbers, wet and dry rot and that the caulking is in good condition.

Defects in painted hulls can indicate problems underneath, so splits in the paintwork are often the first thing to look out for.

Check the rudder for wear and damage, particularly the bearings, which need to be checked for up and down as well as sideways play. Transom hung rudders connect to the hull via pintles and these should be checked for wear and corrosion.

Propellers need to be checked for damage to the blades, including pitting and blade tip damage. The shaft bearings need to be checked for up and down movement plus fore and aft movement and the bracket that supports the prop shaft also needs checking for wear. Also check if the prop anode needs replacing to help ensure the prop stays in good condition.

▼ *The propeller blades here are in fine condition, but the bracket supporting the prop shaft needs to be checked and treated with special anti-foul, and the anode looks as though it needs replacing.*

▲ This boat has been lifted out mid-season to have its hull cleaned and inspected after it made contact with a sandbank – thankfully no damage.

Rig check

A thorough inspection of a yacht's spars and rigging should be carried out at regular intervals by a trained rigger, usually on an annual basis, or at intervals recommended by the manufacturer. The inspection will comprise a visual inspection, sometimes aided by ultrasound tools, where wear is recorded and monitored for future inspections. The inspection will look for items such as cracks in rigging components, misalignment of stays and corrosion. Rig tensions should be checked and adjusted as necessary. A written record should be completed, listing any existing or potential concerns.

Every five years or so, more thorough rig checks should be carried out, which involve disassembly of the rig. This may include Dye Testing or Liquid Penetration Inspections, which reveal surface flaws not visible to the naked eye.

▼ *Regular checks of the rig are essential. It is advisable to deal with any problems as soon as possible and keep a record of when work is done.*

 **CHECKLIST**

- Deck – check split pins, adequacy of threaded fittings, chafe or breakage of stranded wires, rig cracking, rust streaking, condition of mast collar sheaves, halyard alignment, halyard chafe guards, forestay condition.
- Masthead – halyard sheaves rotate freely and are sound, bushes, split pins intact, electrical wires are clamped correctly and are chafe-free, lights are operating, halyard shackles in good condition, Windex and wind gear operating correctly.
- Forestay – roller furling headstay, halyard leads at correct angle to swivel car, inspect halyards for wear on sheaves, fairleads and check swivel cars, mast tang pin hole, corrosion around mast tangs, threaded fittings, no broken strands of wire, signs of cracking or rust.
- Mast stay wires and mast fittings – no broken strands of wire, no visible signs of cracking along swage section, no signs of rust streaking, T-bar plates have retaining plugs or locking tabs, corrosion around mast tangs, fastenings secure, threaded fittings are sound, rigging screws locked.
- Spreaders – no visible signs of cracking, fastenings secure, no signs of rust streaking, broken wire strands, lights are working, wires clamped correctly, no chafe, no corrosion,
- Gooseneck, vang and knuckles – check for signs of corrosion, split pins are protected to safeguard sails, fastenings secure, excessive wear or elongation of fittings.
- Chainplates – check for excessive wear on spacers or bushes, signs of elongation in pin holes, alignment with stay angles, evidence of fracture at deck level, are fastened securely below deck to the hull.
- Spinnaker pole ring – attachment points secure, signs of corrosion around mast tangs.
- Insulators – check for sunlight degradation of plastic insulators, aerial wire securely fastened and in good condition.

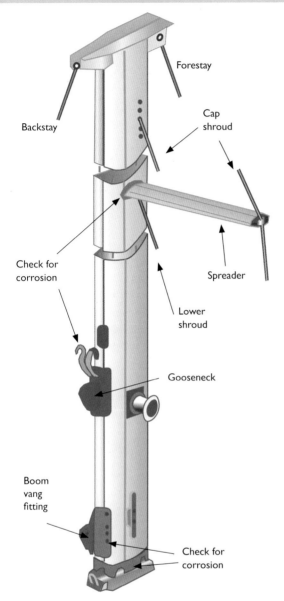

Forestay

Cap shroud

Backstay

Check for corrosion

Spreader

Lower shroud

Gooseneck

Boom vang fitting

Check for corrosion

▲ The main parts of a mast. Leave nothing to chance and do regular visual checks to avoid rig failure.

▼ Headsail furling gear needs regular greasing – an easy but necessary job.

▲ These rigging screws look OK, but the left-hand one is showing signs of rust. Get a professional to take a look.

▼ Check all blocks are aligned properly and run smoothly to prevent chafing of the running rigging. These look fine.

Ground tackle

Anchoring skills and the different types of anchor are covered later in the book – see pages 72–75.

Care and maintenance of ground tackle needs to be considered well in advance of going afloat, to prevent any nasty surprises that might occur when it is first put to use in the season.

Secure stowage of an anchor is vital, as if it is not firmly held in place it can cause damage to a locker or the hull in rough weather.

Before going to sea, check that the fastenings between anchor chain and warp are all in good condition and that there are no signs of chafe in the warp or corrosion of the chain or fastenings. Check that the shackle pins are securely wired on. The best type of warp is nylon rope, as it is slightly elastic and can absorb shocks well.

▼ *This Bruce anchor looks in good condition and is neatly stowed on the bow. The downside of a Bruce anchor is that it does not hinge flat and is awkward to stow on deck.*

Double-check it is well spliced to the chain with no chafe; an eye splice around a thimble that is shackled to the chain is perhaps the best way to attach the two together.

You should know how much chain and warp you have available and it is a good idea to mark the chain with brightly coloured cable ties along its length to help with measuring out the cable when laying an anchor.

If you are planning a cruise, check that you have the right types of anchor on board for the cruising grounds you plan to cover, plus sufficient length of cable for the deepest water you are likely to need to anchor in.

There are several different types of anchor, all designed to suit the different types of seabed including mud, sand, rock and weed. Most yachts carry more than one type of anchor, but again you should check your anchors are suited to your planned cruising grounds.

▼ A completely rusted up shackle between chain and warp has been supplemented by a new stainless steel one here. It is probably time for a complete overhaul of this tackle to avoid mishap.

▲ Before going to sea, ensure your boat has plenty of anchor chain. These anchored yachts are being subjected to strong winds and choppy conditions. To stay securely anchored in a depth of 5 metres they need at least 25 metres of chain.

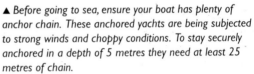

▲ On larger boats, the anchor windlass is a vital piece of equipment which needs to be checked thoroughly before going to sea.

Engine checks

Boat engines on the whole are pretty hardy, but they all need regular inspection and servicing, as recommended in operator maintenance manuals. Engine failure is the most common cause of pleasure craft rescues at sea, for both power and sailing cruisers. Rescue service records confirm that many breakdowns could have been avoided if engines had been checked prior to departure.

Regular examination of an engine helps to identify problems at an early stage, so reducing the risk of engine failure. There is a great diversity of marine craft and engines, so it is essential to have an operator's maintenance manual on board for your vessel's engine, together with the engine's service history. The performance of engines depends on the use of the correct fuels, lubricants and inhibitors and it is important to follow the recommended procedures for winterising and laying up as recommended in the manual.

The golden rule that applies to all engines is to carry out regular engine checks.

▲ *Black powder around the alternator indicates that the alternator belt is not properly adjusted on this engine. This is easily remedied and should be tightened in line with the manufacturer's recommendation.*

Engine problems at sea can often be remedied by working through a problem's possible cause and solution. A good operator's manual should advise what to do if an engine does not start, the starter motor does not turn, the engine overheats, vibrates or makes unusual noises. Skippers who are prepared for such an eventuality should be able to sort out most problems without having to call for help.

Interior

As well as the engine, the interior of a boat has a number of systems that need to be carefully checked annually for wear, deterioration and leaks. Some need to be done on a more regular basis. Often this means reaching into awkward spaces and cavities, so these are jobs that unsurprisingly get ignored by the less agile, but for peace of mind and general safety on board they do need to be done to prevent potentially hazardous, even catastrophic, situations from occurring.

Pre-start, check:
- Fuel levels for main and reserve tanks
- Batteries are fully charged
- For signs of oil, fuel or water leaks
- Engine oil level
- Gearbox oil level
- Prop shaft stern gland is greased (if fitted)
- Engine belts for wear and tension
- Engine hoses for signs of perishing or leaks
- Impeller for signs of wear
- Fuel filter for dirt or water
- Seawater cooling filter is free of debris
- Seawater cooling seacock is open
- Coolant levels of freshwater systems (if fitted)
- Loose wiring

Running engine, check:
- Seawater cooling system is flowing correctly
- Engine hoses, cooling and fuel systems for leaks
- Engine has no unusual vibrations
- Alternator belt is not loose

 **TIPS**

- Carry spare engine filters, hoses, gaskets.
- Carry an engine toolkit.
- Make sure you have an engine manual.
- Familiarise yourself with how to troubleshoot common engine problems.

▼ *The failure of a rubber impeller can cause the engine to overheat and break down. All well-equipped boats should carry a spare.*

▼ *The raw water filter and coolant levels need to be checked regularly, as well as the oil. Cleaning the raw water filter only takes a couple of minutes and is an easy but important task. At the same time, check around the engine for any signs of fuel, oil or coolant leaks.*

Seacocks

There are three main types of seacock: ball valves, cone valves and gate valves.

Seacocks are often awkward to get at, awkward to open and close, slightly intimidating and easily ignored. Should they fail, the results can prove disastrous as most are sited well below the waterline, so unfortunately they cannot be ignored if your vessel is to remain safe. If seacocks are always left open and neglected they can eventually seize, which will prove a serious threat to boat safety should a connecting hose fail and the seacock refuses to close.

It is wise to get into the habit of closing all seacocks when the boat is afloat and not in use. It is also a good idea to make sure the open and closed position is clearly labelled for the avoidance of doubt.

▼ *Seacocks often seize up through lack of use, so it is wise to open and close them regularly.*

Servicing seacocks

All through-hull fittings, including seacocks, should be serviced at least once a year when the boat is out of the water.

Ball valves are hard-wearing, but can stiffen and seize if they are not kept greased, which will also make them more likely to corrode. If a ball valve has become very stiff or seized, the first thing to do is use penetrating oil to try to loosen it. Even if the valve is moving reasonably satisfactorily, it will still pay to take it apart and check it for corrosion, give it a clean and apply fresh waterproof grease to help keep it in good working condition.

If on inspection the valve looks seriously corroded, then be prepared to replace it with a new one, even if it is still working, as trouble could be brewing.

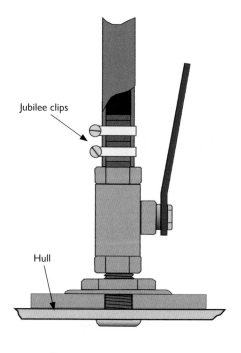

Jubilee clips

Hull

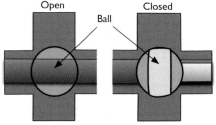

Open   Closed

Ball

▲ *Ball valve*

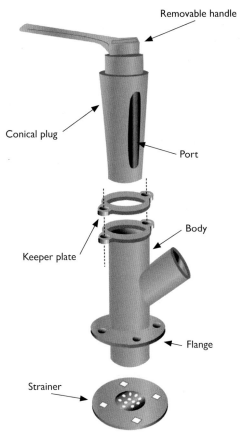

Removable handle

Conical plug

Port

Body

Keeper plate

Flange

Strainer

▲ *Cone valve*

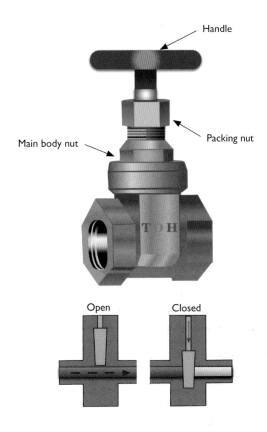

Handle

Packing nut

Main body nut

Open   Closed

▲ *Gate valve*

Cone valves are usually made of bronze, having a conical tube or plug that fits inside a cylindrical body, which connects to a hose. The plug has a hole in one side and as it is turned by a handle the seacock is opened and closed. Although bronze is hard-wearing, the plug needs to be kept greased so that it can turn smoothly and to prevent corrosion.

The plug is held in place by a keeper plate with two bolts and locking nuts, which need careful adjustment to allow the valve to operate smoothly.

Gate valves should also be greased and inspected annually. They are usually made of brass with a circular handle connected to a threaded rod, which moves up and down to open and close a gate in the valve. They are more prone to failure than cone and ball valves, being very susceptible to corrosion in the marine environment. The handles can get very stiff to operate and if they seize they will most

likely need to be replaced. A big drawback with gate valves is that there is no way of knowing whether the valve is open or closed when it is seized.

TIPS

- Make a note of where all seacocks and through-hull fittings are located.
- Ensure all hoses attached to seacocks and through-hull fittings have two stainless steel hose-clips.
- Tie a tapered softwood plug to each seacock and fitting. Plugs can be hammered into a hole in case of a fitting failure.

International Standard
The international standard for metal seacocks and through-hull fittings is ISO 9093-1:1998. When replacing a seacock, check the replacement complies with this standard. Substandard fittings are more likely to corrode and fail.

Gas system

There are correct types of hose for plumbing, sewerage, exhaust, cooling and gas and all hoses should be checked regularly for wear and deterioration. Hose clips should also be checked for corrosion. Nowhere is this more important than with the gas system, so it is essential to check on the condition of the piping and clips. If there are any signs of corrosion, cracking or leaking in the pipes or flexible hose, then these should be replaced immediately.

Gas bottles should be well secured in their lockers and gas drains left unobstructed. Don't be tempted to use the gas locker for extra stowage, as this could result in a blocked gas drain. The gas stove should have no signs of corrosion and burners need to be in full working order, including their safety cut-outs. You can't be too careful with gas, as leaks are very hard to detect until it is too late.

▼ A gas system aboard a boat must follow safety guidelines to minimise the risk of fire or explosion. This includes a secure locker with drain, shut-off valves in the locker and alongside appliances, gas alarms and the use of correct pipework and tubing.

▲ A gas alarm is a useful safety device. It is a good idea to regularly pump the bilges to avoid any build-up of gas and to keep air flowing through the cabin.

▲ This is a secure, purpose-designed gas locker at the stern of the cockpit.

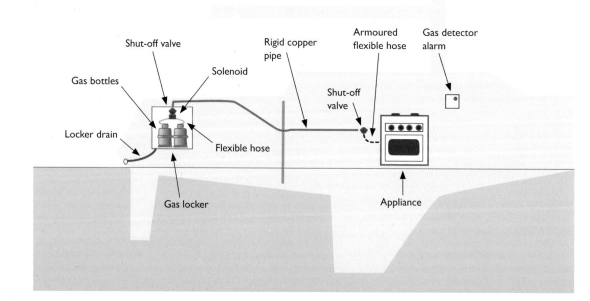

Electrical system

Electrical systems are especially vulnerable when water is close by, so a boat's wiring needs to be protected from water as much as possible. Corrosion can occur easily because of the damp conditions, leading to an inefficient system or even complete loss of contact and equipment failure. Consequently, the wiring and electrical connections need to be checked throughout the boat. Wiring should be multi-strand type to reduce the risk of breakage but if single-strand wiring is used, it would be wise to inspect it for potential failure from time to time and even replace it if time and funds allow.

All wiring needs to be protected from movement to avoid chafing of the insulation. If insulation shows signs of melting then this indicates that the circuit has been overloaded. Unless you are especially knowledgeable, this would be the time to ask an electrician to check over the electrics for you and rectify such problems.

▼ Cruising yachts have complex electrical systems, which don't like being exposed to damp, salty air or being bounced up and down in rough conditions. Check around the boat from time to time to ensure wires and connections are not loose or corroded.

The batteries should be checked and kept in good condition. They should be clamped securely in place to prevent any movement in rough conditions, not only of the batteries themselves but also of the main supply cables. If there is any corrosion around the connections then there will be a drop in voltage, so keeping the connections greased and tightly secured will prevent this.

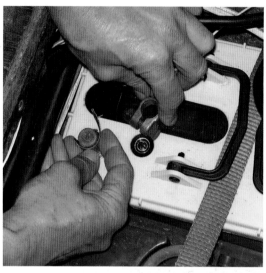

▲ These batteries are in good condition, well-secured with straps to hold them in place and with clean terminals.

Safety briefings and checklists

Before giving your crew a safety briefing, it is worth considering the specific circumstances of the planned trip, the experience of the crew and their familiarity with the vessel and each other.

If the crew already know the drill inside out and you know each other well, then the safety briefing can be limited to a discussion of the passage plan for the day, when and how you plan to leave the berth and the watch-keeping rotas.

If members of the crew do not fully understand the safety drill and do not know where the safety equipment can be found on board, then you will need to brief them on this before departure. It is a good idea to have a safety briefing checklist at

▲ Make sure all the crew know where the seacocks are and where the safety equipment is stowed, including emergency equipment.

▼ Before departing on a cruise, do a visual check of all the boat's equipment and systems, working through a checklist to make sure nothing is forgotten.

hand so you can go through everything in detail. The items to cover include location of safety equipment, use of gas stoves, what to do in the event of fire, actions for man overboard and abandoning ship.

Ensure that at least one of the crew in addition to yourself can operate the radio and knows the routine for sending distress signals. Also, remember to ask the crew if any of them are on medication and give out seasickness tablets if necessary.

If you have very young or novice crew aboard, then have a quiet run through with them and leave nothing to chance. The secret here is not to alarm inexperienced crew in any way and to reassure them that the boat is not going to heel over and sink as soon as it leaves the harbour.

Keep a positive attitude and don't dwell on the likelihood of gas explosions, but on the great time everyone is going to have out on the water.

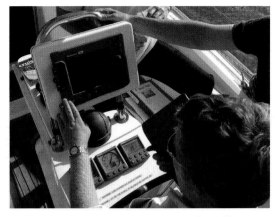

▲ Do a run through of the instruments and navigation equipment.

▼ On deck, run through the safe operation of winches, clutches, mast controls and the anchor.

Safety Briefing Checklist

Down below:

- Lifejackets and harnesses – fitting, when to wear, clipping on
- Gas – risks, precautions, gas bottles and taps
- Fire prevention – extinguishers, fire blanket, where and how to use
- Moving around – companionway, handholds, galley safety
- Heads – how to use
- Seacocks – location of
- Hatches – opening and closing, risks
- VHF – how to use
- Engine – basic operation
- Batteries – location

On deck:

- Hazards – boom, tripping, slipping, hatches
- Clipping on – jackstays
- Heaving line
- Engine controls
- Instruments
- Lockers – contents
- Winches and clutches – safe operation
- Anchor – safe operation

Emergency:

- First aid – kit location
- MOB – equipment – throwing line, horseshoe buoy, dan buoy
- Flares – where, when and how to use
- VHF – emergency procedure
- EPIRB – how to activate
- Liferaft – where, when and how to launch
- Grab bag – where, contents
- Steering failure – emergency tiller, where and how
- Flooding – seacock failure, plugs, bilge pumps, bailing procedure

Welfare:

- Seasickness – what to do, how to avoid
- Food and drink – use of galley
- Kit – stowage
- 'One hand for you – the other for the boat!'
- Concerns

Safety equipment

Safety equipment is an important part of boat preparation and you need to make sure that your vessel is properly equipped. There are strict laws for commercial vessels and for pleasure vessels over 13.7 metres in length but no statutory requirements exist for pleasure vessels under 13.7 metres in length other than those stipulated in SOLAS V.

While you should be mindful of any laws that exist in your country regarding pleasure boat safety, it makes sense to keep your vessel appropriately equipped and for that equipment to be serviced and up to date. Many boatowners are put off doing this because safety equipment can be costly and might never be used. It is tempting but unwise to ignore safety equipment expiry dates.

Here are some lists of safety equipment recommended by the UK's Royal Yachting Association, with essential, mandatory and recommended items for vessels up to 13.7 metres and over 13.7 metres in length.

Pleasure vessels up to 13.7m in length
Essential:
- Lifejacket (or buoyancy aid) for all on board
- Safety harnesses (varies with type of boat)
- Kill cord and spare (varies with type of boat)
- Marine radio (VHF)
- Chart(s), almanac and pilot book
- Hand-bearing compass
- Handheld white flares or powerful torch (for collision avoidance)
- 406 MHz EPIRB/PLB (varies with area of operation)
- Distress flares
- First aid kit
- Liferaft and grab bag (varies with area of operation)
- Firefighting equipment
- Equipment to deal with a man overboard (life ring, dan buoy etc)
- Emergency tiller (for wheel-steered boats) (varies with type of boat)
- Equipment to deal with water ingress (bailer, bilge pump, bungs)
- Bucket (strong with lanyard)
- Emergency VHF aerial for fixed VHF (varies with type of boat)
- Anchor and cable/warp
- Tools and spares (engine, electrics, rig, sails)

▲ Although there are no strict laws about wearing lifejackets on pleasure vessels, it makes sense to wear them and to be ready to clip on safety harnesses in rough conditions.

- Boarding ladder
- Spare fuel
- Waterproof torches
- Mooring lines and fenders
- Knife
- Pump and puncture repair kit (for inflatable boats)
- Alternative means of propulsion (oars, outboard engine etc)
- Ship's log book
- Accurate clock or watch

Pleasure vessels up to 13.7m in length
Mandatory:
- Radar reflector
- Lifesaving signals
- Navigation lights, day shapes and sound signalling equipment

Pleasure vessels up to 13.7m in length
Recommended:
- LW radio
- Fixed steering compass (lit at night)
- Drawing instruments for navigation (plotters and dividers)
- Binoculars
- Echo sounder
- Log
- GPS/chart plotter

- Navtex
- Barometer (varies with area of operation)
- Storm sails (for sailing yachts) (varies with area of operation)
- Bosun's chair (for sailing yachts) (varies with type of boat)
- Tender
- Tow rope
- Boat hook

Pleasure vessels up to 13.7m in length
At your discretion:
- MF/HF radio (varies with area of operation)
- SSB radio and/or satellite phone (varies with area of operation)
- Automated Identification System (AIS)
- Radar
- SART/AIS SART (varies with area of operation)
- Propeller guards and rope cutters
- Sea anchor and/or drogue (varies with area of operation)

Pleasure vessels over 13.7m in length
Essential:
- Lifejacket (or buoyancy aid) for all on board
- Safety harnesses
- Kill cord and spare (varies with type of boat)
- Chart(s), almanac and pilot book
- Hand-bearing compass
- 406 MHz EPIRB/PLB (varies with area of operation)
- Distress flares
- First aid kit
- Emergency tiller (for wheel-steered boats)
- Equipment to deal with water ingress (bailer, bilge pump, bungs)
- Emergency VHF aerial for fixed VHF (varies with type of boat)
- Anchor and cable/warp
- Tools and spares (engine, electrics, rig, sails)
- Spare fuel
- Waterproof torches
- Mooring lines and fenders
- Knife
- Pump and puncture repair kit (for inflatable boats)
- Alternative means of propulsion (oars, outboard engine etc)
- Ship's log book
- Accurate clock or watch

Pleasure vessels over 13.7m in length
Mandatory:
- Radar reflector
- Lifesaving signals
- Navigation lights, day shapes and sound-signalling equipment
- Marine radio (VHF)

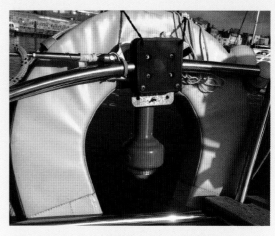

▲ *Ensure all crew are familiar with how life rings are quickly deployed. Fumbling about for a few extra seconds in a man overboard situation could prove disastrous.*

- MF/HF radio (varies with area of operation)
- Handheld white flares (for collision avoidance) or powerful torch
- Liferaft and grab bag (varies with area of operation)
- Firefighting equipment
- Equipment to deal with a man overboard (life ring, dan buoy etc)
- Bucket (strong with lanyard)
- Boarding ladder

Pleasure vessels over 13.7m in length
Recommended:
- LW radio (to receive BBC Radio 4 shipping forecast)
- Fixed steering compass (lit at night)
- Drawing instruments for navigation (plotters and dividers)
- Binoculars
- Echo sounder
- Log
- GPS/chart plotter
- Navtex
- Barometer
- Storm sails (for sailing yachts)
- Bosun's chair (for sailing yachts)
- Tender
- Tow rope
- Boat hook

Pleasure vessels over 13.7m in length
At your discretion:
- SSB radio and/or satellite phone
- Automated Identification System (AIS)
- Radar
- SART/AIS SART
- Propeller guards and rope cutters
- Sea anchor and/or drogue

Passage planning

A well-prepared passage plan can make the difference between a safe, trouble-free trip or an experience that could prove unenjoyable and possibly hazardous.

Passage planning helps you to:

- Decide where to go.
- Calculate how long it will take to get there.
- Avoid bad weather.
- Take advantage of favourable tides.
- Be aware of possible hazards, eg shipping lanes, tidal overfalls.
- Decide a watch system.
- Decide if the crew is experienced enough for the trip.
- Be prepared to react in case of emergency.

When planning a passage, small-scale charts are used to create an overall strategy. This helps the skipper and crew consider such factors as the most efficient route, alternative routes and possible ports of refuge in case of emergency. Large-scale charts are needed for destinations and hazardous areas of the route.

If going outside your country's territorial waters, make sure you have original documents on board including ship's logbook, registration certificate, insurance, radio licence, International Certificate of Competence and courtesy flags for your destination.

Keeping charts up to date

Keeping up-to-date charts is an important safety consideration which is often overlooked by leisure sailors but considered an absolute priority by professional navigators. A chart that has not been updated can be as dangerous as not having a chart at all. Publishers of paper and electronic charts provide chart correction information and services online. Updates and corrections are made available as Notices to Mariners (NMs) which are available online for free. Guidance notes for accessing UKHO Admiralty Chart updates can be found on the UKHO website at www.ukho.gov.uk/nmwebsearch/.

 **TIPS**

- Carry large and small-scale paper charts in addition to electronic navigation aids.
- Carry pilot books that provide harbour information and passage notes for your cruising area.
- Study the tidal heights and streams and make notes to cover the whole trip.
- Check on customs regulations if applicable.
- Check you have all necessary documents.

▼ *When planning a trip, spend time ashore reading almanacs and pilot books and studying charts. Make notes of your plans and share them with your crew well in advance of departure.*

TIPS

Contingency plan

- Before going to sea, it is always a good idea to make a contingency plan in case conditions deteriorate unexpectedly or there is a problem with your vessel or a crew member is injured.
- Ensure you could navigate safely to places of refuge without the need of electronic aids, in case of power failure.
- Make a note of the tidal predictions at the emergency destination, to be sure of accessibility.
- Make sure someone ashore knows of your plans and how to raise the alarm if they become concerned for your well-being.

◀ As you near destinations, once again run through pilotage books and make sure the crew are clear how to enter harbour safely. And keep a running log.

▼ Marks ashore to aid navigation could prove meaningless to the uninformed. Here the boat is heading into a narrow entrance and safely lined up with the two marks on the headland.

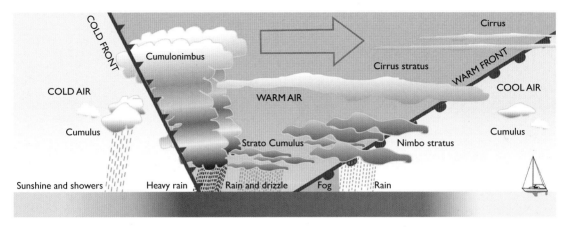

▲ This section through a depression has wind moving from left to right. High cirrus is followed by layers of cloud which gradually become lower as the warm front passes, bringing rain. Thick stratus cloud in the warm sector is followed by heavy rain and eventually cumulus cloud appears, eventually giving way to sunshine.

Weather forecasting

A competent sailor will have a good basic understanding of how to interpret a weather forecast. Most weather forecasts present a general picture of what to expect in your area over a given period of time. We rely on such forecasts to provide basic information, but the actual weather and sea conditions we experience don't always tally with the general view. This is not necessarily the forecasters' fault, as it is the local tides, topography and sea breezes that interact with this basic picture and give rise to the actual conditions we experience out on the water. To make more accurate predictions of the weather in your specific area requires more in-depth knowledge and skill.

It is up to the skipper to make a calculated interpretation of the available forecasts and to decide whether it is safe for their vessel and crew to go afloat. A major part of making that decision is done through observation and being able to assess where in the forecast weather pattern you actually lie. Has that predicted front passed through yet, what are the clouds telling you, what is the wind strength, how has it changed through the last few hours and what is the barometer doing? Study your charts and estimate when and where you can expect wind against tide. Are the elements going to clash severely and if so when is this going to happen? Will you need to avoid being in that area or will the conditions be manageable?

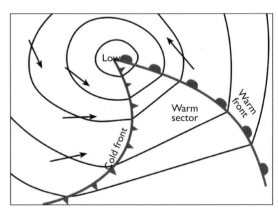

▲ A typical depression in the northern hemisphere moves in an anticlockwise direction with low pressure in the centre.

Sources of weather forecasts

To help reach your decision, it is best to gather as much reliable information as you can. Sources of weather forecasts include:

- National meteorological offices
- Internet – good source for GRIB forecasts (Gridded Information in Binary files), eg UGrib, weather charts, web services eg Windguru, also back-up to VHF, NAVTEX, INMARSAT-C and SSB radio
- MSI (Marine Safety Information) broadcasts on VHF and SSB radio
- Public service broadcasts on radio and tv
- NAVTEX, Weatherfax and INMARSAT-C
- Harbour and marina offices
- Local knowledge – talking to locals in the know, for example fishermen, can help you decide

▲ *A cold front is approaching with towering cumulus and heavy rain. Squalls such as this are commonly accompanied by high winds exceeding 20 knots.*

Caution: The internet is not part of the MSI system and should never be relied upon as the only means to obtain the latest forecast and warning information. Access to the service may be interrupted or delayed from time to time, updates may also be delayed. Refer to GMDSS services, INMARSAT SafetyNET or NAVTEX for the latest information. When using these web pages, check that the page on your screen is not from your cache. Use the Refresh button to update if in doubt.

Compare a number of pressure charts to see how the weather patterns have been forecast to evolve in your area over a number of days. This will help you to judge when fronts will pass through, what local conditions will be as a result and how this tallies with your planned departure and route plan.

Terms used in weather forecast bulletins

General synopsis – how, when and where weather system is moving

Fair – no significant precipitation

Backing – wind is changing in an anticlockwise direction

Veering – wind is changing in a clockwise direction

Barometric pressure and tendency:
Steady – change less than 0.1mb in 3 hours
Rising or falling slowly – change 0.1–1.5mb in last 3 hours
Rising or falling – change 1.6–3.5mb in last 3 hours
Rising or falling quickly – change 3.6–6.0mb in last 3 hours
Rising or falling very rapidly – change more than 6.0mb in last 3 hours
Now falling/now rising – change from rising to falling or falling to rising within the last 3 hours

Visibility:
Good – greater than 5 nautical miles
Moderate – 2–5 nautical miles
Poor – 1000 metres to 2 nautical miles
Fog – less than 1000 metres

Sea state:
Smooth – wave height 0.2–0.5m
Slight – wave height 0.5–1.25m
Moderate – wave height 1.25–2.5m
Rough – wave height 2.5–4.0m
Very rough – wave height 4m+

Strong wind and gale warnings:
Strong wind – if average winds are expected F6–F7
Gale – if average winds are expected F8+, gusts 43–51kn
Severe gale – if average winds are expected F9+, gusts 52–60kn
Storm – if average winds are expected F10+, gusts 61–68kn
Violent storm – if average winds are expected F11+, gusts 69kn+
Hurricane force – if average winds are expected F12+

Timing:
Imminent – within 6 hours from time of issue
Soon – within 6–12 hours from time of issue
Later – more than 12 hours from time of issue

Before you go

Always study the weather forecast thoroughly before going afloat in order to remain safe and to make an efficient passage plan. Before departure, download forecasts to cover the anticipated length of your passage. Be prepared to delay your departure or change your destination if the weather forecast is unfavourable.

Once committed to going, ensure that you have the means to get regular, reliable weather forecasts if you are at sea for any length of time. This will allow you to change your plans and head for a safe haven if the forecast is for stormy weather, and to take advantage of detailed weather information when planning your route.

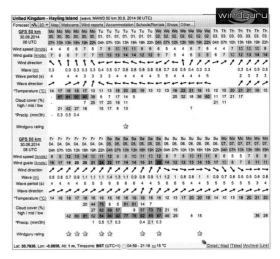

▲ Windguru is an excellent website that gives accurate hourly predictions for popular windsurfing locations. Also very useful for inshore sailors.

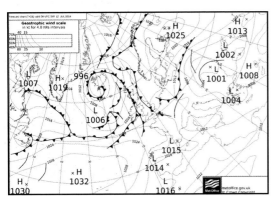

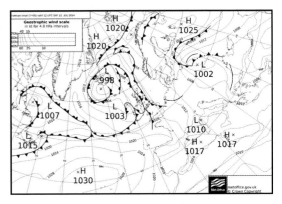

• This sequence of four synoptic charts predicts the weather over a 36-hour period. The circular lines are isobars, joining areas of equal barometric pressure. Air moves from high to low pressure. Isobars that are close together indicate stronger winds. Isobars that are further apart indicate lighter winds.

• The lines with triangles and semi-circles represent fronts. Warm fronts are shown with semi-circles and cold fronts with triangles. The way in which the semi-circles and triangles point shows the direction in which the front is moving.

• In terms of the wind direction, in the northern hemisphere air moves around high pressure in a clockwise direction and low pressure in an anticlockwise direction, so isobars indicate the direction and speed of the wind as well as the pressure.

• Where a cold front and warm front meet, an occluded front is created, shown by lines with overlapping semi-circles and triangles. Black lines with no semi-circles or triangles are troughs and show areas where the air is unstable and showers tend to form.

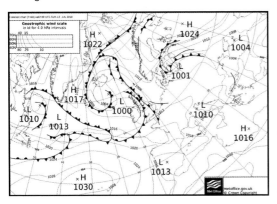

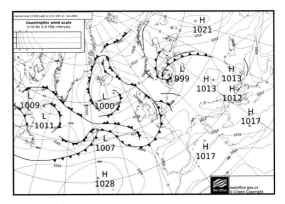

TIPS

- Study the Beaufort scale and use it to judge wind strengths.
- Practise how to interpret barometric pressure charts.
- The barometer is arguably the most useful forecasting tool. Keep a note in the log to monitor change in barometric pressure.
- Learn how to observe cloud formations to forecast the weather.

▲ Onshore sea breezes develop as the land heats up during the day and cumulus clouds often form. Here, a good breeze is developing on a summer's afternoon with clouds over the land.

Beaufort Scale

Force	Knots	Sea State
0 Calm	Less than 1	Sea like a mirror.
1 Light air	1–3	Ripples with the appearance of scales are formed.
2 Light breeze	4–6	Short wavelets. Crests do not break.
3 Gentle breeze	7–10	Large wavelets, crests begin to break. Scattered white horses.
4 Moderate breeze	11–16	Small waves, becoming longer, frequent white horses.
5 Fresh breeze	17–21	Moderate waves, many white horses. Chance of some spray.
6 Strong breeze	22–27	Large waves; white foam crests more extensive everywhere, spray likely.
7 Near gale	28–33	Sea heaps up, white foam from breaking waves begins to be blown in streaks. Much spray.
8 Gale	34–40	Moderately high waves, longer, edges of crests begin to break into spindrift. Well marked streaks of foam.
9 Severe gale	41–47	High waves, dense streams of foam. Crests begin to topple, tumble and roll over. Spray may affect visibility.
10 Storm	48–54	Very high waves, long overhanging crests. Whole surface of the sea white. Tumbling of the sea heavy and shock-like. Visibility affected.
11 Violent storm	55–62	Exceptionally high waves. Sea completely covered with foam. Edges of crests everywhere blown into froth. Sea completely white with driving spray.
12 Hurricane	63+	Air filled with foam and spray. Sea completely white with driving spray. Visibility very seriously affected.

▲ *Launching a tender from this slipway is a strenuous, messy business at low water but easy at high water.*

Understanding tides

If you are used to sailing in tidal waters, you will know that tides can be both a benefit and a hindrance to the sailor. In many ways, the benefits far outweigh the disadvantages as tides can offer the navigator a free ride, provided they have correctly factored the high and low water times into their passage plan. If a trip does not go to plan, then being caught in an adverse tide can seriously slow you down.

For those not so familiar with sailing in tidal waters, here's a guide to the basics. Tides are the rise and fall of the sea level caused by the gravitational pull of the Moon and the Sun on the Earth. As the sea levels rise or fall, a flow of water or tidal stream results, creating a horizontal movement that flows backwards and forwards according to the height of the tide. The frequency, heights of sea level and speed of the tidal streams vary considerably around the Earth's surface. Detailed data are available to the navigator in tidal atlases, charts, nautical almanacs, mobile applications and online.

Tides vary according to the relative positions of the Sun and Moon and their combined influences on the Earth's oceans.

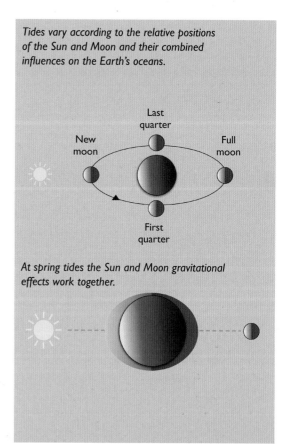

At spring tides the Sun and Moon gravitational effects work together.

Basic principles

To understand the basic principles of when and how tides and tidal variation occur, it helps to study how the Moon orbits the Earth and in turn the Earth rotates on its axis as it orbits the Sun (see diagram).

Some vital statistics which are useful to know:

- Each orbit of the Earth by the Moon takes 27.32 days.
- The Earth takes 24 hours to do one rotation on its axis, and 365 days to orbit the Sun.
- Due to the cyclic rotation of the Earth and Moon, the tidal cycle is 24 hours and 50 minutes long. During this period there are either two high tides and two low tides, or one high and low, depending on your location. Every 14 days the Sun, Moon and Earth are lined up or 'align'.

When the alignment of the Sun, Moon and Earth happens, the gravitational pull of the Sun and Moon on the Earth are at their greatest, resulting in spring tides. At spring tides, the heights or range of high and low water are at their greatest

and tidal streams will reach their fastest speed. As the Sun and Moon fall out of alignment, the effect of their combined gravitational pull weakens until they are at right angles to each other. At this point neap tides occur, when the tidal range is at its lowest and the tidal streams will flow at their slowest. Other factors also come into play to further complicate how tides behave, but it helps to grasp these basic principles in order to understand the forces at work.

Around the coasts of north-western Europe and the east coast of North America, tides occur twice daily. These are known as semi-diurnal tides. In these regions, there are two high tides and two low tides every 24 hours 50 minutes.

The Pacific coasts of North America have two highs and two lows per day with considerable variation in the first and second tides, which are known as mixed tides.

Around the coasts of the northern Gulf of Mexico, much of the Pacific and Australia, the tides are mostly diurnal, ie once daily, having one high and one low tide per day.

▼ Water depths and drying heights on charts are measured above chart datum, which is the lowest level the tide is ever expected to fall. Estimating the tidal heights at any given time and place requires analysis of data from tide tables to help calculate the tide times and heights at a specific time. Charts are needed to provide the exact position and its charted depth.

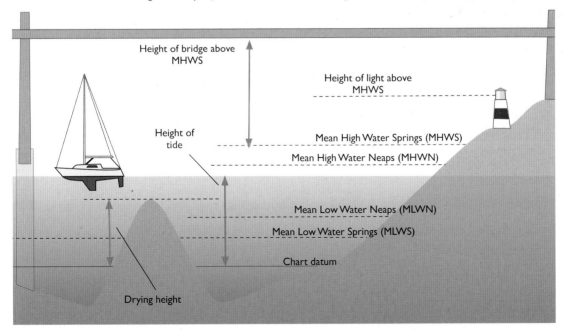

Tidal range

The tidal range at any given place on the Earth's surface varies enormously, according to coastal topography, depth of water and size of the sea or ocean. Exceptionally high tidal ranges occur along the coasts of oceans and in bays. The greatest tidal range is found in the Bay of Fundy in Canada (15.25 metres), whereas seas such as the Baltic and Mediterranean experience little or no tide at all, due to their smaller volume and size compared to the oceans.

Tidal streams

The tidal stream is very important for the navigator and at any given location it continuously changes. The direction of the stream, known as the set, and its strength, known as the drift, change through time as the tide falls, or ebbs, towards low water and rises, or floods, towards high water.

The good news for the navigator is that the tides behave in a predictable manner at any given location and detailed information is available in

▼ *The direction and speed of tidal streams are heavily influenced by headlands, islands and the nature of the seabed, sometimes resulting in circular flows that can catch out the unwary. It is always a good idea to study tidal atlases when passage planning.*

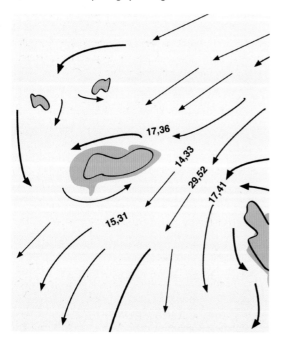

17,36
14,33
29,52
17,41
15,31

TIPS

- Double-check all calculations
- Remember to allow for Summer Time, if applicable
- Avoid shallow water on a falling tide

almanacs, charts and tidal atlases to assist them with their task.

When planning a trip in tidal waters, always check the tides before going afloat. Use almanacs, charts, tide tables and tidal stream atlases to gather all the data you need. It is advisable to have a written note of tidal data for your trip including:

- Your boat's draft
- The predicted times (in Universal Time) of high and low water
- The heights of the tide
- The tidal ranges
- The direction and speeds of the tidal streams en route

Check when and how the state of the tide will affect local areas including shallows, harbour entrances, sand bars, headlands and estuaries.

Also check predictions and forecasts to determine if and when rough seas caused by wind against tide will occur. Be prepared to change your plan to avoid being caught in adverse conditions.

Use all the data you gather to:

- Plan your departure time(s)
- Take advantage of tidal flow to shorten journey time
- Estimate your journey time
- Plan your arrival time(s)
- Avoid potential hazards caused by tidal conditions
- Ensure there will be safe clearance under your keel at all times

▲ Navigating tidal estuaries requires plenty of planning and is a rewarding experience if everything goes to plan.

▲▼ The same position seen at high and low water clearly shows that this starboard lateral mark in Chichester Harbour, UK has been placed right at the edge of the channel and leaves no margin for error. Navigators choosing to go inshore of lateral marks should always double-check the height of the tide and their draft, even when they are well offshore.

2 BOAT HANDLING

On-board communication, leadership and teamwork

As a skipper you need to have complete and constant awareness of everything that is happening with the boat, including sail trim, navigation and pilotage, other vessels, potential breakages, changes of weather, crew welfare and more.

In effect it's an executive oversight of what's happening both on board the boat and in its vicinity. You also have to look ahead in time, figuring out what's liable to happen in the future and how to deal with likely challenges you may face.

However, the natural inclination of many who are new to skippering is to get stuck into actively sailing the boat – in other words, tasks the crew should be undertaking. This makes it difficult to maintain that constant awareness and monitoring that is vital to safe skippering. Instead you tend to become preoccupied with the task, whether it's hoisting sail, reefing or steering. When this happens the skipper can quickly lose all perception of the big picture of what's going on around the vessel, and indeed even what's happening on board.

Never underestimate the extent to which getting involved with crew work will diminish a skipper's ability to keep abreast of everything that's happening with the boat. A key problem is when something unexpected happens during the task in hand, for instance reefing lines and sail battens getting snagged when hoisting the mainsail. When this happens, it seems to be human nature to focus on the immediate task in hand to the exclusion of everything else.

It's therefore really easy for a two- or three-minute job to turn into one that is the sole focus of your attention for ten minutes or more, during which you don't look properly around outside the boat. By this time the boat may have moved close to a mile from its original position and a ferry may have left its berth and be coming up right behind you.

Crew management

Effective crew briefings are a vital part of the good on-board communication that helps everything to run smoothly. Involving everyone on board, including children, with sailing the boat will also make the experience more satisfying for all and, equally importantly, maximises the chances of remaining a motivated team if conditions start to get tough. This process starts with formal briefings, but we all know how little retention we have of many of these.

It's therefore also important to brief everyone on the water before each manoeuvre. When hoisting the mainsail, if everything goes perfectly it may feel as though it's easier to just get on with doing it yourself; however, it only takes a few moments to talk through the procedure first:

'Jo will take the sail ties off, working forwards from the back of the boom, and then stand at the mast ready to bump the halyard up. Once she's there we will slow down, I'll let off the mainsheet and Claire will turn the boat to point into the wind. When I give the signal, Jo will start hauling the sail up and Pete will tail the halyard at the companionway.'

This simple explanation gives even those with minimal sailing experience a clear vision of what's going to happen and what their role will be. At the same time, you're free to keep an eye open to spot any problems at an early stage.

Preparation and planning

These are key elements of effective skippering that help to identify potential hazards and reduce the time you will need to spend on navigation and pilotage. Time spent below with your head in the chart, pilot book or tide tables is time that you're not in tune with what's happening up on deck, so as part of your planning make sure you have all the information you might need at your fingertips.

Even for a short day sail, returning to initial home port, you should have a clear understanding of the weather and tidal patterns for the day, as well as knowledge of any local regulations that may be

▲ A good skipper will run through the day's plan with the crew prior to departure.

in place. On a longer passage it's also important to have a plan B that you can execute in the event that it doesn't go according to expectations. This plan should include ports of refuge accessible from your expected route.

Don't let events overtake you

Relaxed skippers think ahead and are prepared for a wide range of eventualities. However, there may still be times when things start to happen too fast, with a risk that events will overtake the rate at which the skipper can cope with them.

A common example of this is a tricky pilotage situation, potentially at night, when it's critical to recognise times at which the boat is travelling faster than you can navigate. The obvious solution, slowing down, often does not come to mind in such situations, but reducing speed from say 5 knots to 4 knots gives a lot more thinking time than the 20 per cent difference in speed suggests. There may even be occasions when it's helpful to stop for a short while – so that you can catch up with events and get ahead.

A variety of strategies to buy additional time when necessary is therefore one of the most useful elements in a skipper's armoury. Heaving to, furling (or partially furling) the headsail, and stemming the tide are prime examples.

All the above is not to say that good skippers don't enjoy a stint on the helm, taking part in deck work when in open water or, for instance, preparing a meal under way, but it's important to recognise that these tasks are secondary to

▼ *Make sure each crew member knows what to do as you prepare for each manoeuvre.*

their skippering role. However, if you're sailing short-handed, maybe with only one other crew member, there are times at which the skipper will need to be more involved with sailing the boat, which poses additional problems.

Short-handed sailing

This is the default situation for many crews, whether it's a choice to sail predominately as a couple, or if you have children that are too young to be fully fledged crew members and may even need a degree of looking after while you're under way.

If sailing short-handed you will need to find more space and time for manoeuvres and make sure you pause any task in which you're involved to look around, ideally at least every minute. This will ensure your overall situational awareness is up to date and that you haven't missed anything important that's developing either on board the boat or in its environs. This could include increasing wind requiring a reef, a ship on a potential collision course or a wind shift that puts the boat at risk of a gybe.

Even so, when multi-tasking there's a danger of focusing on one task to the detriment of others. A digital stopwatch with a loud alarm every minute is therefore a useful aid that will prompt you to get in the habit of always making time to check around the boat.

▼ *Don't expect a novice to helm like a pro. Gentle words of advice are more effective to help build confidence rather than a continual barrage of commands.*

Watch-keeping

The effects of sleep deprivation are not to be underestimated as they quickly lead to severely impaired capacity for flexible and innovative thinking, exaggerate tendencies to take risks, and reduce motivation. All these factors have a negative impact on a skipper and crew's ability to handle the boat safely.

Even on a long day sail, it's worth making sure each person can get some rest to help avoid fatigue and ensure everyone on board has reserves of strength to tackle unexpected problems. As little as an hour and a half can make a noticeable difference if your return to port is significantly delayed. Similarly, on a longer passage in which a formal watch system needs to be operated it's equally important for crew members to start getting rest as early as possible on the first day.

At the best of times sleep can be difficult on the first night at sea, so it's worth considering being a little flexible with the length of watches, especially with a small crew, and making them relatively short, possibly as little as two hours. On subsequent nights at sea it's easier to sleep and watches can be longer, allowing each person time to get deeper sleep. The difficulty of sleeping on the first night is what makes 24–36 hour passages so tough. However, beyond that you fall into a regular sleep pattern and it's not unusual for crews to arrive in port after a week at sea better rested than at the start of the voyage.

Sleep cycles

Having some understanding of sleep patterns is a prerequisite to making effective use of your time off watch. Normally, we have four or five 90-minute sleep cycles every night. If we wake naturally at the end of a cycle we'll feel relatively refreshed, but not if woken mid-cycle. Two watches below every 24 hours, each with three hours spent in the bunk, is therefore a minimum, assuming the time is actually spent sleeping.

Two hours off watch is enough for one cycle, allowing time to remove foul weather gear, use the toilet and so on, and this may be what you

▼ Watch systems can vary according to the length of voyage and number of crew. Traditional watches use periods of four hours on, four hours off. Here are two variations each with two watches.

	1	2
0000 - 0400	OFF	ON
0400 - 0800	ON	OFF
0800 - 1300	OFF	ON
1300 - 1900	ON	OFF
1900 - 0000	OFF	ON
0000 - 0400	ON	OFF
0400 - 0800	OFF	ON
0800 - 1300	ON	OFF
1300 - 1900	OFF	ON
1900 - 0000	ON	OFF

	1	2
0000 - 0400	OFF	ON
0400 - 0800	ON	OFF
0800 - 1200	OFF	ON
1200 - 1600	ON	OFF
1600 - 1800	OFF	ON
1800 - 2000	ON	OFF
2000 - 0000	OFF	ON
0000 - 0400	ON	OFF
0400 - 0800	OFF	ON
0800 - 1200	ON	OFF
1200 - 1600	OFF	ON
1600 - 1800	ON	OFF
1800 - 2000	OFF	ON
2000 - 0000	ON	OFF

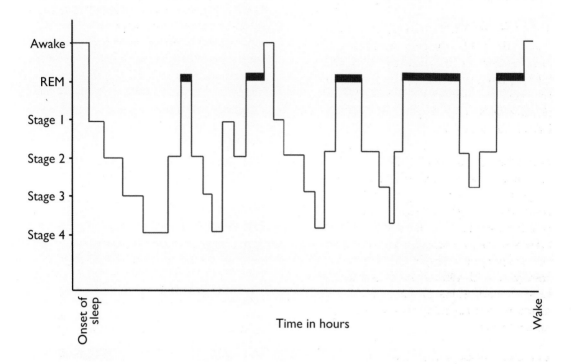

▲ The chart shows the characteristics of a normal adult sleep pattern. The stages of sleep include REM (rapid eye movement) when the brain is active and the body paralysed; Stage 1 (sleep drowsiness) progresses through Stages 2, 3 and 4 (deeper stages of sleep). The time spent in REM is shown by the solid blue bars.

need to aim for on the first night at sea. However, three-hour watches may involve waking the off-watch crew mid cycle, when they will awaken groggy and tired. It's also worth harnessing the power of short naps – a couple of 20-minute spells with your head down during the day can make a big difference to alertness levels.

Nutrition

This is just as important as getting decent sleep. On a boat, especially in heavy weather, we tend to use a lot more energy than in a relatively sedate desk-bound life on shore. Lack of food will similarly result in confused (and sometimes confrontational) thinking and severely reduces motivation. Make sure you eat early when on passage, eat well and eat often – and don't forget to drink plenty, especially if the weather's very hot, or if you've been seasick.

There are times when it pays to be aware of impending worsening conditions – for instance, a more uncomfortable sea state when the wind turns against the tide, or when moving out from

behind the shelter of a headland – and adjusting eating times accordingly to maximise your chances of getting (and keeping) the meal down.

Although night watches are frequently very rewarding, cold can creep up on you slowly during an extended watch, so keeping warm is a key factor in staying alert. A supply of snacks, preferably carbohydrate-based items, will give a continuous release of energy, rather than a sugar-induced peak, followed by a sleep-inducing slump.

Watch for other crew members who may be at risk of succumbing to seasickness – withdrawing from activity and conversation are typical signs of someone who's feeling ill. Remember that this often goes hand in hand with a lowering of body temperature. Sufferers frequently decline to go below, worried about the adverse effect of being below deck, but once horizontal in a bunk with their eyes closed most people are OK, with their nausea slowly subsiding and body temperature gently rising.

Principles of collision avoidance

The obligations of each vessel, however small, to avoid collisions are laid down in detail in the International Regulations for the Prevention of Collisions at Sea (IRPCS). A core overriding principle is that each vessel must maintain an effective lookout at all times, both for boats that are nearby and for those that may be several miles away but could be approaching quickly.

The next stage is to establish whether a risk of collision exists. If so, the give-way boat (which is carefully defined by the IRPCS) should give a clear indication of her intended action to avoid a collision. However, there is no such thing as a 'right of way' boat – the other vessel also has clearly defined obligations to avoid collision.

The IRCPS also sets out six different categories of craft – power-driven vessels, sailing boats, vessels constrained by draft, vessels restricted in their ability to manoeuvre, vessels towing and those engaged in fishing or trawling. There are therefore many situations in which, even if you're under sail, you have to give way to ships. This is particularly true if they are navigating what to them is a narrow channel in the approach to port, or in clearly defined traffic separation schemes at sea. To be on the safe side, skippers should know the IRPCS and keep a copy aboard.

In practical terms it also behoves skippers to avoid close-quarters situations in the first place – the more you push your luck as stand-on vessel, the bigger the risk of a collision occurring.

▼ Before crossing a shipping lane, remember to let approaching ships pass and then cross as quickly as possible on a heading at right angles to the lane. In light winds, it is best to use the engine.

Night sailing

The well-publicised loss of the 25-foot yacht *Ouzo* after collision with a ferry south-east of the Isle of Wight highlights many of the dangers associated with navigation at night. Even in good visibility, a standard 10-watt navigation light for a yacht of less than 12 metres (40ft) is visible for little more than one mile. A ship travelling at 20 knots will cover that distance in just three minutes. Equally worrying is that the range of navigation lights is significantly reduced when a boat is heeled more than 10 degrees.

One of the most chilling aspects of the loss of *Ouzo* is that until six minutes before the collision, the *Pride of Bilbao* ferry was on a course to overtake, passing well clear of the yacht. Over the following three minutes, however, the ferry made a slow course change in excess of 20 degrees, bringing the two vessels onto a collision course. This highlights the need for a constant all-round lookout at all times, and to monitor all other vessels – even if they don't appear to be a threat – until they are well past and clear. As well as the blind spot under the genoa, remember that it's very easy to forget to regularly look astern. The latter point is all too easy to forget when you're straining at identifying navigation marks ahead of your boat.

At night, as well as keeping a white handheld anti-collision flare to hand, it's worth keeping a powerful cordless searchlight that can be used to illuminate the sails on deck at night.

▼ Keep a constant all-around lookout when night sailing and leave nothing to chance. Double-check that the light you are looking at is coming from the mark you think it is and navigate with extra caution, especially if you are tired.

Importance of a balanced sail plan

Even the most talented and experienced of crew will struggle to steer the boat efficiently if the sail plan is not well balanced. Therefore, paying careful attention to sail trim and shortening sail in good time as the wind increases is crucial to the ease of steering the boat. This also improves the vessel's motion and increases her speed. Don't underestimate the extent of the effect each sail has on the steering of the boat: powering up the mainsail will help you luff up towards the wind, while depowering the main by letting the sheet out while keeping power in the headsail will help to bear away.

Sail shape

It's also important to ensure the boat is not over-powered, as this has a significant effect on steering, with the boat wanting to head up into the wind, especially in big gusts. Before the wind reaches a strength in which you need to reef, sails can be depowered by increasing the tension in halyards, plus the mainsail clew outhaul and cunningham. Increasing backstay tension has a similar effect, especially on boats that are fractionally rigged.

In gusty conditions many yachts will also need to have the mainsheet eased in the puffs in order to be able to maintain a reasonably straight course, otherwise the extra power will tend to spin the boat up into the wind.

▶ *The telltales on this headsail are all flowing horizontally, showing this boat is well set up in 12 knots of breeze.*

Boats with ageing Dacron sails are at a particular disadvantage, as the old cloth will stretch in a strong wind, making the sails even baggier, which reduces forward power, while also creating significantly more heel. By contrast, a flat sail shape will minimise heeling while still giving a large component of forward drive.

Dacron vs laminate sails
On a windy day, if you get the opportunity to compare two boats that are otherwise identical, but with one having Dacron sails and the other a laminate suit, the difference in the handling of the two vessels with the wind forward of the beam is very instructive.

The behaviour of the two in gusts is the most revealing aspect. The laminate sails will maintain their shape, enabling the boat to continue in a straight line and at much the same speed, with

maybe a couple of degrees of extra heel and marginally more weather helm for the duration of the gust.

However, the handling of the boat with Dacron sails is liable to be very different. Each time a gust hits, the sails will physically stretch, taking on a deep and baggy profile. This in turn increases heel by as much as 10 degrees, causing the boat to broach up into the wind. As well as the difficulty in handling the boat associated with this, it will lose speed, so you will be at sea for longer, and it makes the boat more uncomfortable for everyone on board.

What's most noticeable in these photos is that the luff of the Dacron headsail is much baggier than with the laminate genoa. In both cases these photos are of new sails – older Dacron sails can be expected to stretch considerably more.

▼ The laminate headsail holds its shape well and is better at withstanding gusts than the Dacron sail.

▼ The Dacron headsail here is much baggier than the laminate sail and will not perform as well as the laminate sail.

Reefing

The wind strength at which you will need to shorten sail varies between different boats and even between the same boats with different sails. However, there's one universally helpful guideline when it comes to figuring the right time to reef. Even experienced skippers tend to do so too late, so the old adage 'when you think you need to reef, it's already too late' is worth following.

An efficient and effective mainsail reefing system will make any boat easier to handle, as well as making it faster and safer, as you will feel more inclined to put a reef in as soon as it's needed. Many owners, especially of larger yachts, solve this by fitting in-mast furling. However, this comes with a number of drawbacks including complexity, a lot of additional weight aloft (which reduces stability) and compromised sail shape.

On the other hand, if a conventional slab reefing system is well optimised, one competent person working alone should be able to tuck in a slab reef on any boat up to around 40 feet in roughly 60–90 seconds without undue effort. With electrically powered winches this can realistically be achieved on boats of 50 feet, even for those who are well beyond the first flush of youth.

The problem is that many reefing systems are not well designed, with excessive friction a common problem, and many are configured so that one person has to work at the mast, while another is back in the cockpit. It's much better to either have everything, including halyard and reefing pennants, handled at the mast, or everything at the companionway, including pennants that will pull the luff cringles neatly down to the gooseneck. The former has the advantage of simplicity and minimising friction, while the latter means the sail can be reefed without leaving the safety of the cockpit.

Roller bearing batten car systems in place of the slides on the luff groove also help to significantly reduce the effort associated with raising and lowering the mainsail on a larger boat. In many cases they can also enable reefing to take place with the apparent wind aft of the beam, which

reduces the apparent wind strength. Acceleration gear is also often needed in extreme conditions – either lots of wind, or very little – when it's difficult to get the boat moving. This is achieved by sailing a little off the wind, with sheets eased to suit and with slightly fuller sails, with cunningham and outhaul eased if the acceleration gear is to be used for any period of time. Once the boat is close to sailing at its normal speed for the conditions, you can sheet in and flatten the sails a little, effectively changing to a higher gear to achieve a faster speed.

It's worth taking time to make a reef as neat as possible – you'll be repaid by better performance, which means less time spent at sea in the bad weather and the boat will handle better as well.

▼ *A deeply reefed main on this training vessel in 20 knots of wind allows the boat to remain well under control and easy to handle.*

▼ *This boat is under control but if it is hit by a heavy gust it could well become over-powered and the crew will need to react quickly.*

CHANGING GEAR

Just as with riding a bike, it helps to be able to change gear on a boat to suit different conditions. This is done by altering sail shape. An acceleration gear, for instance, is useful when sailing upwind in waves, when each wave will tend to slow the boat. It can also be helpful tacking in confined waters, when it can take anything up to a full minute to build up to normal speed.

Dealing with challenging tides and currents

Big tides demand considerable respect and require a greater degree of planning to ensure that you don't allow them to work against you, as well as creating the potential for a confused sea state in wind against tide conditions. However, with careful timing a big tide can also be used to your advantage, either to considerably speed progress towards your destination, or to allow you to take useful short cuts if the water level is sufficiently high.

Nevertheless, strong and complex tidal streams are one of the biggest challenges in some parts of the world. For instance, spring tides on the south coast of the UK can run at up to 4 knots, and even stronger rates are possible in parts of northern France and the Channel Islands, as well as around other significant headlands. In places where tides set strongly, many displacement craft will need to time their passages for a favourable

▼ *Sailing against a fast flowing tide in light airs is not desirable. Here, the tide is going to be the winner.*

stream in this area, while planing powerboats will need wind with tide on account of the steep seas generated in wind against tide conditions.

However, the stream is rarely a uniform mass of water moving at a constant speed in a uniform direction. Instead, it's weaker in shallow water and near the shore, and at its fastest in deep water. The core principles are that the tide runs fastest in deep water, while relief from an adverse stream can be gained in shallow water. In addition, the stream in shallow water and in bays will frequently change direction before the main stream — in effect the edges turn first, which can start very early as a back eddy, before the main stream follows in the new direction anything from 30 minutes to as much as three hours later.

Wind and tide effects

The direction of the wind relative to the tidal direction has a significant impact on sea state. If both are flowing in the same general direction, the sea will tend to be flattened out, while wind against tends to produce a short and steep sea that can be very tiring, even if the stream is helping you make excellent progress towards your destination.

▲ This skipper has headed inshore to take advantage of a back eddy that is flowing close to the shore while further out the tide is still flowing strongly in the opposite direction.

Cross tides

In a strong cross tide it's all too easy to be swept downtide of the rhumb line between your starting point and destination. In an area such as the Solent, between the mainland and islands off the Brittany coast, where distances are very short, GPS can be used to ensure you track in the correct direction.

However, there's also an easy solution for boats without electronic aids: use a hand-bearing compass to keep the mark behind you on a bearing that will lead you to the next mark. It's very simple and very accurate and if you're able to line up a couple of marks on shore that are on the correct bearing you can do it all by sight.

Longer legs, taking more than an hour or so, in which the strength or direction of the tidal stream changes significantly, will need a different approach. Here a course to steer calculation that allows for the net tidal flow you will experience is more efficient than constantly adjusting course as the stream fluctuates.

Tidal races

These tend to form off headlands, where the tidal rate is accelerated and the seabed is liable to be very uneven, often with a significant underwater ridge. As a result, it's possible to get disturbed water even in almost calm conditions and they can be positively dangerous, even to ocean-going yachts, in wind against tide conditions in anything more than a moderate breeze.

A race can be avoided by staying a few miles offshore in moderate conditions and more in severe weather; however, the exact distance necessary varies with different headlands – look for the symbols on your chart for overfalls and tide races. It's also important to consult local pilot books, which will provide more detail about each significant headland and what can be expected there in different conditions.

In some cases, in good to moderate conditions smoother water often exists very close inshore – this passage is up to half a mile wide, but can reduce to 50–100 metres as the wind increases

▲ Use a hand-bearing compass to keep the mark behind you on a bearing that will help lead you to the next mark.

▼ On a long passage, following a track that involves continual course alterations due to the ebb and flow of tides takes much effort and can result in a journey time that will be longer than necessary.

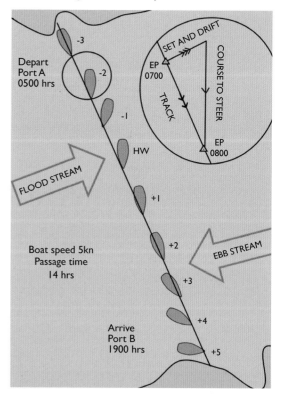

Depart
Port A
0500 hrs

-3

-2

-1

HW

+1

+2

+3

+4

+5

FLOOD STREAM

EBB STREAM

SET AND DRIFT

EP 0700

TRACK

COURSE TO STEER

EP 0800

Boat speed 5kn
Passage time
14 hrs

Arrive
Port B
1900 hrs

and may vanish completely in poor conditions. Again, pilot guides will indicate whether such an inshore passage is available and, if so, which stages of the tidal cycle the stream will flow in each direction.

A similar situation can arise with sand bars at a harbour entrance. With a strong onshore wind and ebb tide, these have the potential to form dangerous breaking waves in shallow water. In such cases it's invariably safer to stay at sea in bad weather than it is to risk entering the harbour.

Tidal gates

The speed of an adverse tide at some headlands effectively turns them into tidal gates that you won't get past unless the stream is flowing in the correct direction. Clearly, a similar situation also exists with bars and harbour entrances and harbours that have restricted tidal access.

If possible, time your passage so that you aim to get to the tidal gate an hour or so before it

opens. You're much more likely to arrive there later than expected, rather than earlier, so this approach maximises the chances of getting through unhindered.

Tidal heights

Be extra careful when you're sailing near low water on spring tides as there may be a lot less depth than you expect for an hour or so each side of low water.

Pay particular attention to areas that, because they're never exposed – and are therefore shown on charts as blue, rather than green – can all too easily catch the unwary.

Some of these in popular sailing areas may have least depths of only 0.6m below datum well offshore. They are therefore covered by a reasonable depth for maybe 98 per cent of the time, but for an hour or two on a few days once a fortnight will be too shallow for any yacht to pass over.

▼ *A well-planned course here shows that the shortest distance is not the track, even though the course to steer is the same as the track, because the flood and ebb tides cancel each other out over the passage.*

▼ *Course planning, where a fast-moving yacht steers a course quite different from the track and makes the fastest possible passage.*

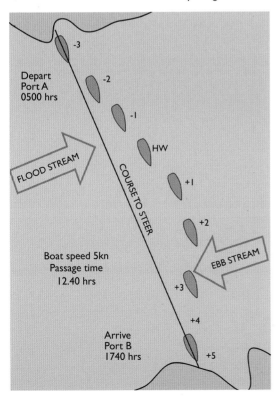

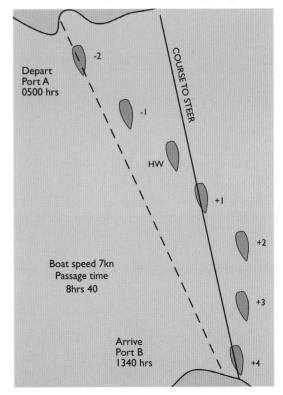

▲ *Sailing upwind, a good helmsman makes constant adjustments for changes in wind direction and wave condition.*

▼ *After the boat tacks, a good helm will build speed by bearing away a little before luffing back up to windward.*

Sailing to windward

Few sailors relish the prospect of a passage to windward, especially in stronger winds. Given the boat's motion is likely to be unpleasant and passage times may be some 25 to 40 per cent longer than with a free wind, this is not surprising. However, there's a lot that can be done to make the boat faster and more comfortable.

One of the most common mistakes is to point too close to the wind. If you're not an accomplished racing helm and don't have a race prepared boat, it's almost always faster to bear away 5–10 degrees, ease the sheets a fraction and aim for increasing boat speed at the expense of a super-close angle to the wind.

The reduction in leeway will instantly give you back half the angle, while your speed may increase by as much as 20 per cent. The boat will also be easier to steer and many will not slam as much into the waves.

Wind shifts

The wind never blows from a constant direction. Instead it will either oscillate every few minutes each side of an average direction, or will have a tendency towards a permanent slow swing in one

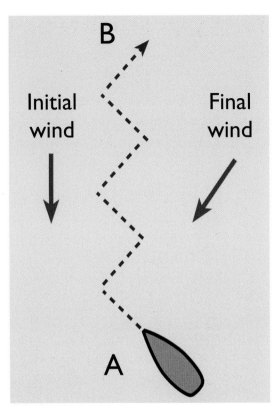

▲ *If the wind were only to blow from one constant direction, then making short, evenly spaced tacks upwind would be the ideal track to follow.*

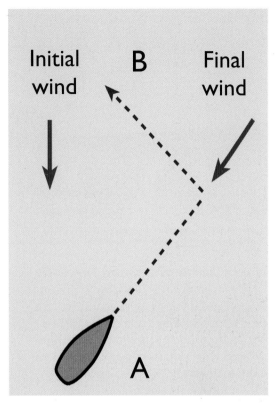

▲ *If wind shifts can be correctly anticipated, or are forecast to occur, then taking advantage of them will result in an easier and quicker upwind passage.*

direction or the other. Both these effects can be harnessed to make a windward passage faster.

With an oscillating wind, if you tack with the biggest wind shifts you may gain up to 20 degrees in terms of direction, simply by making sure you're on the favoured tack as much of the time as possible. For instance, if you're beating against a wind that is, on average, from a northerly direction, you will benefit from being on port tack when it backs west of north and on starboard tack when it veers east of north.

Traditionally, racing sailors would remember their average course on each tack, but figuring out which tack is favoured is much easier now that some chart plotters display a graph of historic wind data for up to one hour.

A different strategy is needed if the wind is swinging (or forecast to swing) in one direction. Here we're not really interested in any short-term oscillations; instead, if we simply start on the tack that takes us towards the new wind

direction, when the big wind shift comes we will be on the favoured tack and may even have the advantage of a free wind.

For instance, if you know that a northerly wind will swing into the north-east, start out heading in that direction on port tack. If you then tack on to starboard when the wind shift arrives, you'll have an easy sail to your destination. However, a boat that started out at the same time on port tack will again be directly downwind of the destination port after the wind shift.

Cross tides on longer windward passage

In a similar fashion, it's possible to use changing tidal streams to your advantage if they are roughly at right angles to the direct line to your destination. Start out by sailing on the tack that will make your ground track align more closely with the rhumb line, then tack when the tide changes direction. This can significantly shorten a windward crossing of the English Channel or southern North Sea.

◄ Keeping a hull clean and polished helps improve performance, especially in the case of boats such as this with long, deep keels.

▼ The dirty bottom of this yacht is affecting its performance, though most would agree that the cost of lifting out and scrubbing it is not yet justified.

Importance of a clean bottom

One of the easiest ways to boost windward performance is to make sure your boat has a clean bottom, as even a thin coat of slime is like towing a bucket behind the boat. By the time green weed starts to grow, the frictional resistance of the hull will be increased by as much as 20–30 per cent.

Given enough power, whether from sails or engine, you may still be able to reach a respectable top speed, as wave-making resistance starts to greatly outweigh friction. However, when sailing to windward you're never at top speed and reducing frictional resistance is a much larger part of the overall equation.

Headsail reefing

Unfortunately, large overlapping furling genoas are not efficient if you're trying to sail with the wind well forward of the beam in a strong breeze. The problem is that once the genoa has been furled by more than a few turns the luff becomes very baggy, which reduces the boat's ability to point close to the wind and increases heel without a corresponding increase in drive.

There's no doubt therefore that more modern rigs, with a small non-overlapping jib rather than a large overlapping genoa, are easier to configure for sailing upwind efficiently in a range of conditions. Decent reefing systems will tame the mainsail easily, while the jib won't need many rolls to reef down to almost storm jib size.

▲ A deeply furled overlapping genoa is reducing the ability of this boat to sail upwind. A smaller jib would be a lot more efficient.

However, many older boats can be successfully modified by changing to a non-overlapping jib and then adding a longer boom to give more mainsail area. This might be expected to increase weather helm; however, much of the area of an overlapping genoa behind the mast is also aft of the centre of lateral resistance and therefore contributes to weather helm.

Heavy weather jibs

An alternative is to fit an additional removable forestay, just behind the main one, on which a separate small jib can be set. This can be a powerful arrangement, especially with a sail designed specifically to be at its optimum in heavy winds, and also makes setting a storm jib easy as it can be hanked to the same stay.

In the past such removable inner forestays were all made of stainless steel rigging wire, but the development of materials such as Dyneema, a polyethylene, from which rope as strong as steel can be produced, means this is now frequently used for the purpose.

Motor sailing

It's not surprising that this is a popular move if you have a good distance to travel to windward. In many cases it can give a useful boost to boat speed and allow you to steer closer to the wind than otherwise. However, don't be tempted to steer directly into the wind as the boat will be slowed by taking waves head on and if the mainsail is allowed to flap this increases drag, as well as damaging the sailcloth.

There is, however, a drawback to relying on the engine for a windward passage in heavy weather. The motion of the boat is likely to disturb any sediment that would otherwise be sitting on the bottom of the fuel tank, with the result that this can block the fuel filters after a period of time and stop the motor.

▲ A well-balanced sail combination here with a jib and reefed main makes for easy helming in 20 knots of wind.

▼ Having a second forestay has enabled this yacht to furl in its genoa and hoist a jib, keeping it well balanced. If the wind increases they could easily set a storm jib, leaving the furled genoa in place.

Surviving heavy weather, towing drogues

Some crews seem to be able to take heavy weather in their stride, when others struggle, even when sailing more capable boats. So what does it take to make light work of heavy weather?

Sail selection and trimming

Whatever your boat, stretched and baggy sails inevitably make heavy weather more difficult to handle, as the amount of drive they produce is reduced, while the poor sail shape increases the angle of heel. Similarly, deck gear that doesn't allow easy trimming of the sails also makes it difficult to keep them set efficiently. Don't underestimate the impact of these effects – for a start, steering becomes more difficult and the boat's motion will be more uncomfortable.

Unfortunately, roller-furling sails, especially headsails with UV-strips, are at their most baggy when well reefed. It's therefore worth having a smaller heavy-weather jib that can be set from a separate removable inner forestay. This sail can be cut very flat and complements a well-set double- or triple-reefed mainsail, allowing the boat to be sailed at near maximum efficiency in strong winds below the level that would require use of the storm jib.

Using the engine

In practice, many cruising boats use engines to help make progress to windward in bad weather, allowing them to point closer to the wind and make better speed, with less leeway. This can be a very effective strategy, especially when heading around 20 degrees to the apparent wind, with a deep-reefed mainsail.

There is, however, a potential problem, as these are exactly the conditions in which any dirt in the fuel tank gets stirred around. Therefore, blocked fuel filters are a common occurrence in bad weather, especially on a boat in which the tank has not been cleaned for several seasons. Fitting parallel primary filters in the same way that is commonplace on many motor boats and big yachts makes it possible to switch to the second filter in a matter of seconds in the event of the first becoming blocked.

▲ Sailing in heavy weather is challenging but also very exhilarating as long as the crew are prepared and well coordinated.

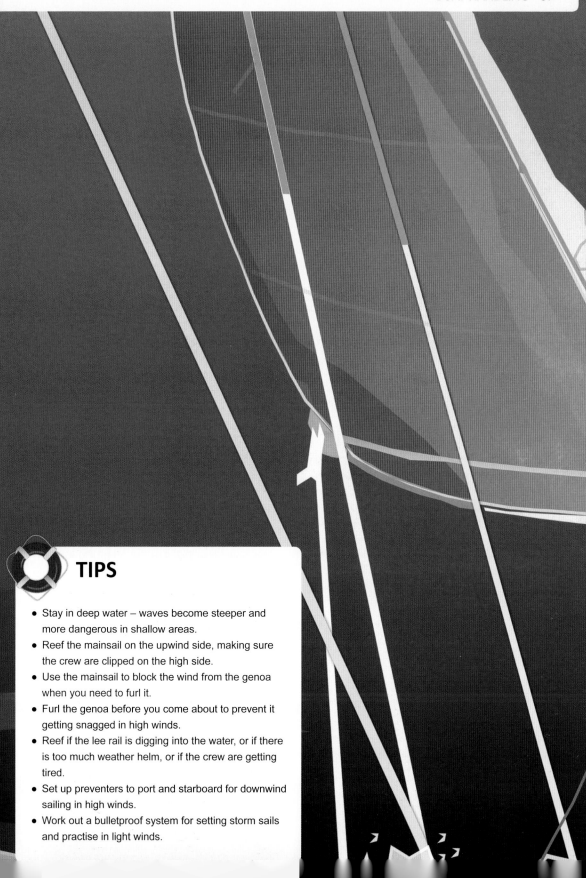

TIPS

- Stay in deep water – waves become steeper and more dangerous in shallow areas.
- Reef the mainsail on the upwind side, making sure the crew are clipped on the high side.
- Use the mainsail to block the wind from the genoa when you need to furl it.
- Furl the genoa before you come about to prevent it getting snagged in high winds.
- Reef if the lee rail is digging into the water, or if there is too much weather helm, or if the crew are getting tired.
- Set up preventers to port and starboard for downwind sailing in high winds.
- Work out a bulletproof system for setting storm sails and practise in light winds.

Boat handling

Wind angle is the biggest factor that will determine your strategy in heavy weather. With the wind well forward of the beam, many boats will require some mainsail (or trysail) to be used, until the point at which the boat is fully powered up with just a small jib. With the wind on or aft of the beam, it's worth having a proportionately larger headsail and smaller (or no) mainsail, as this will help prevent the vessel broaching towards the wind. In addition, running before the wind with only the headsail avoids any danger from the boom in an accidental gybe.

In all cases, you should aim to steer the smoothest path between the waves. With the waves forward of the beam, the fastest and most comfortable course is to luff a few degrees towards the wind as the bow rises on each wave, before bearing away a few degrees as the crest passes the boat.

With the wind well aft of the beam, as each wave lifts the back of the boat it will tend to turn the vessel towards the wind, sometimes quite considerably. Turning the bows away from the wind a little the moment before the wave lifts

▼ *Going upwind in rough conditions, bear away down the waves and head up when going up and over the waves.*

▲ *With the wind on the beam, it is best to have a larger headsail and deeply reefed main than the other way around.*

the stern means the boat will tend to continue in a straight line, which both reduces motion and increases speed.

Yielding to the conditions

It's a mistake to think that you always have to fight heavy weather – there may be other strategies that can be employed until the wind starts to abate. All require a degree of sea room – if you're close to a lee shore your only strategy may be to attempt to claw away from the danger.

For most yachts the first stage is likely to be to heave to, with the jib backed and the helm to leeward. This is a strategy that can be employed in any strength of wind, but is also effective under storm canvas in very strong winds. Another

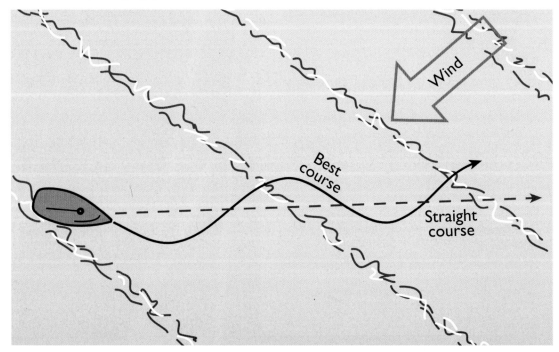

option for many modern boats is to lie ahull, with no sail and the helm tied to leeward – a tactic that can be surprisingly effective, providing there are no breaking waves.

Surviving breaking waves

Most yachts have surprising reserves of stability, until they are presented with breaking waves of a size that have the potential to roll the boat upside down. In open sea these are most likely to be experienced after a big change in the wind direction, such as when a cold front brings an unusually large wind shift. Equally, big changes in depth of water, such as continental shelves and headlands, can precipitate breaking waves.

A boat is most prone to being rolled when lying beam on to the seas, so formation of breaking waves marks the limit of using heaving to or lying ahull as a viable strategy. In most cases the next stage will be to lie to a sea anchor or drogue, which are respectively designed to keep bow or stern pointing into the seas. A sea anchor or drogue can also be employed to prevent a boat running out of sea room – it will significantly reduce the vessel's drift rate compared to heaving to or lying ahull.

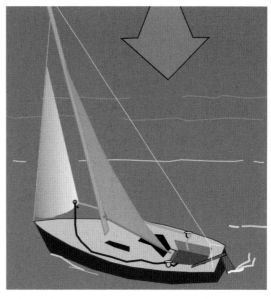

▲ In very heavy weather, heaving to until conditions improve can be the best option.

A further advantage of heaving to, lying ahull or towing a drogue/sea anchor is that the boat requires little input from anyone on board, beyond keeping a good lookout. As a result, crew members should be able to get rest and sustenance, giving them reserves of energy should a crisis develop that needs immediate attention.

▼ Going downwind in rough conditions, head up going down the waves, then bear away going up and over the waves.

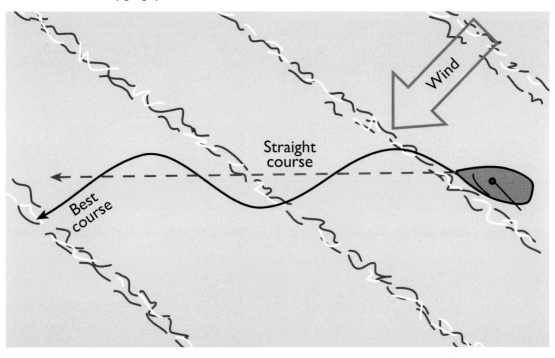

Danger areas

There are some locations in which conditions can reliably be predicted to be worse than those elsewhere. These include wind against tide situations, especially near headlands at which depths change significantly and the wind is also likely to be accelerated.

Never assume that heading for port is automatically a safe solution, as there are many in which the entrance is positively dangerous in strong or gale force onshore winds. Notable examples of these are estuaries or rivers with shallow bars, especially when there is a strong ebb tide running, as well as many man-made harbours.

Mooring

Just as some harbour entrances can be dangerous, there are also places within a port that are not safe to remain in severe weather. When visiting an unfamiliar harbour with storms forecast, choose your mooring location carefully, opting for somewhere where there's as little fetch as possible.

TIPS

Don't let problems escalate

- While this sounds obvious, it's all too easy to overlook in the initial adrenaline rush when events don't go according to plan…
- Know when it's best to yield to conditions, rather than fight them.
- Identify the small number of occasions when you really do need to fight, for instance to claw off a lee shore, or if the boat is taking on huge amounts of water.
- Take care of yourself and the crew, and stay rested.
- Keep a generous margin of safety, especially if there are dangers to leeward.
- Keep track of the situation as it changes and make sure you're always prioritising the right things.
- Keep learning and stretching your skills.

▼ *In heavy weather, make sure you have plenty of oversized fenders and double up lines so that if one breaks there will always be another that will do the same task.*

Personal experience: Rupert Holmes describes his experience of a gale in the Celtic Sea aboard a 29-foot yacht with a short-handed crew.

My first open-sea gale was in the Celtic Sea, midway between Land's End and Mizen Head – exactly where the storm that devastated the 1979 Fastnet Race fleet struck.

A vigorous cold front passed overhead at dusk, leaving a north-north-westerly with mean speeds of 32–35 knots and gusts of more than 40. We pressed on for a while under just a small headsail, the helm nicely balanced and the boat, a relatively lightweight 29-foot cruiser-racer, bouncing enthusiastically over impressive waves.

However, even if the boat didn't break, our small crew stood to be quickly exhausted, given that the tiller pilot certainly wasn't up to handling the conditions. As we had nearly 100 miles of sea room, the decision to stop was an easy one – the only question was how? We already had the mainsail down, so the traditional option of heaving to wasn't an automatic choice, and hoisting more sail seemed like the wrong option. Instead we dropped the headsail and lay ahull,

with the tiller lashed to leeward. The boat immediately stopped bucking and spray stopped flying. Under the pressure of the wind on the rig we heeled to around 15 degrees, sometimes a little more, as a wave passed underneath, and then returned almost to upright.

In contrast, five larger yachts broadcast MAYDAY calls that night and were towed into Kinsale, in south-western Ireland. For us the wind eased the following morning, allowing us to head for Kinsale in a blustery force 6–7, but conditions that the boat, with efficient sails and reefing systems, was well set up to manage.

Clearly taking the strain off both boat and crew was the right thing to do. But what would have happened if the wind had continued to increase and breaking waves made lying ahull risky? This was a pertinent question, given that we had no drogue or sea anchor on board, but after discussion we decided the best option would be to try towing a spare small headsail behind as an improvised drogue sea anchor.

'our small crew stood to be quickly exhausted...the tiller pilot certainly wasn't up to handling the conditions...'

Anchoring

Anchoring is one of the most important boat-handling skills. If you can set an anchor correctly with confidence and know your boat will be safe in a secure anchorage, then you can rest in comfort and will not need to rely on moorings and marinas when cruising. You can also leave your boat at anchor and go ashore safe in the knowledge that the anchor will not drag. If you do not know how to anchor correctly then you risk endangering your boat and also others who might be anchored nearby. And if your anchor is unsuitable for the type of seabed beneath your keel then there is a high chance of the anchor dragging. For some boatowners, the fear of the anchor dragging means they stay awake all night, as a result getting little or no sleep and most likely stressing out their crew into the bargain.

Getting anchoring right is not always straightforward. It can be confusing with the many types of anchor available and there will always be conflicting opinions on which anchors would be best suited for your boat and your chosen cruising ground. Anchors and chain weigh a great deal, so loading up with excessive chain and anchors can affect a vessel's performance and only really be necessary if planning a long-distance voyage along a variety of potentially exposed stretches of coastline.

Types of anchor

Choosing the type and size of anchors and cable to carry aboard will depend on the type and size of your vessel and the sea area it is being used in. Most importantly, choose anchors that are big enough for your vessel and recommended by the manufacturers. Cruising yachts normally carry at least two types of anchor, plus suitable lengths of chain and rope cables.

▼ *Types of anchor*

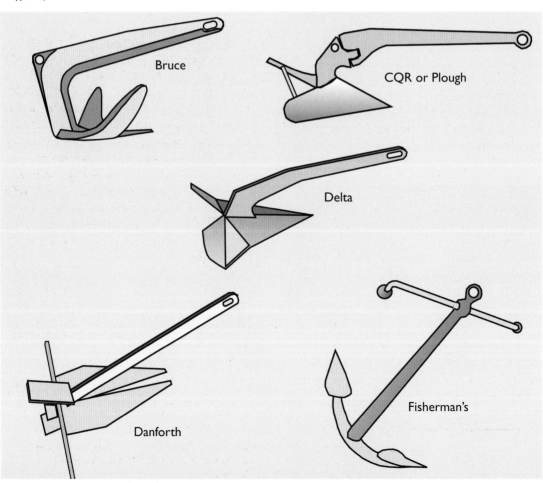

Bruce

CQR or Plough

Delta

Danforth

Fisherman's

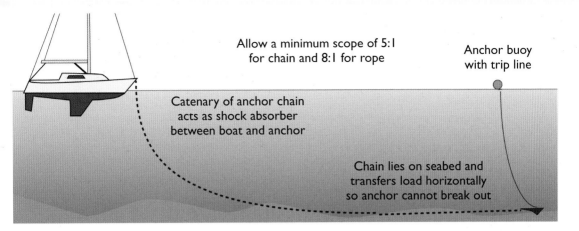

Allow a minimum scope of 5:1
for chain and 8:1 for rope

Anchor buoy
with trip line

Catenary of anchor chain
acts as shock absorber
between boat and anchor

Chain lies on seabed and
transfers load horizontally
so anchor cannot break out

Types of anchor include:

- Bruce – good power to weight, easy to handle, holds well in mud, sand and rock.
- CQR or plough – good power to weight, stows well on bow roller, though awkward on deck. Holds well in mud and sand. Very popular and reliable.
- Delta – good power to weight, also plough shaped. Stows well on bow roller.
- Danforth – stows flat, good kedge anchor, hard to break out of mud. Excellent back up anchor. Prone to pull out if the wind or current reverses.
- Fisherman's – the traditional anchor. Good for rocky and heavily weeded seabeds, but heavy and awkward and not so good in sand and mud.

Chain and warp

Anchor cables can be either chain or rope, or both. For an anchor to work effectively, the vessel's pull on its cable must be parallel with the seabed, otherwise the anchor will break out from the seabed and drag. The weight of chain prevents this from happening, providing there is sufficient length of chain lying on the seabed.

A further factor that helps is the effect of the catenary curve of the cable between the boat and the anchor. This acts as a shock absorber between the boat and the anchor, so if the boat is hit by a sudden gust of wind the cable will straighten and tighten before it pulls hard on the anchor.

Hauling in an anchor and chain can be very heavy work if your vessel lacks an anchor winch, but chain is much stronger and will not chafe on the seabed, unlike rope. A workable solution is to have the anchor cable consist of part chain, which lies on the seabed and part rope, to make it more manageable. An all-rope cable is much lighter and easier to manage, but less secure and prone to chafe. All-rope cables are normally used with kedge anchors.

How much cable should you use? The amount, or scope, depends on the type of cable, the depth of water beneath the keel, plus the weather conditions and the height of tide. If anchoring in calm conditions with little or no tide, the absolute minimum scope for chain is considered to be 3:1 and 5:1 for rope. In light to moderate conditions a ratio of 5:1 for chain and 8:1 for rope is generally accepted and in worsening conditions a ratio of 8:1 for chain and 10:1 for rope. In tidal areas, the rise and fall of the tide needs to be allowed for and if necessary adjustments will need to be made if at anchor for several hours or overnight.

▲ Anchoring is a vital skill for the cruising sailor and also enables access to quiet locations away from the crowds.

Trip line

Most anchors have a small hole for attaching a trip line, for use if there is risk of the anchor becoming fouled. The line is either brought back on board and cleated or connected to a small buoy which floats above the anchor.

Choosing an anchorage

There are a number of factors to consider when choosing a place to anchor. Begin by studying the chart and look for recommended anchorages near your destination, which are marked on the chart with anchor symbols. Look for a location that will be sheltered from wind and waves in as many wind directions as possible and away from any strong tidal streams. Also check the chart to see whether the ground will be suitable for anchoring and make sure you check the charted depths.

You will also need to bear in mind the wind direction and forecast for your planned stay and the state of the tide and tidal streams. Anchoring on a lee shore should definitely be avoided, even if the chart has an anchor symbol on it.

▶ *When anchoring, leave plenty of space between boats in case others have a different cable or scope to yours. These two are quite close and could well get tangled with each other if they need to let out more chain as the tide rises.*

 **TIPS**

- Study charts and almanacs to find a suitable anchorage.
- Consider the seabed (also on charts). Sand or firm mud are ideal.
- Check the charted depth.
- Consider the conditions forecast for your planned stay, especially wind direction and strength – will the anchorage be sheltered?
- Consider the state of the tides – check the rise and fall and calculate the best depth to anchor in. Double-check there will be sufficient depth at low water, and sufficient chain for high water.
- Check the anchorage is well away from strong tidal streams.

▼ *This sheltered bay in Kalymnos, Greece offers complete protection from wind and waves, making for an ideal, safe anchorage – the open sea is beyond the headland to the left. As an added bonus there are no tides to worry about and the bay is not accessible by road.*

▲ *This anchor chain has a safety rope attached inside the locker to ensure the anchor remains held in place when not in use. The deep locker enables the heavy chain to self-stow easily.*

▲ *Electric windlasses are labour saving but use a lot of battery power. It is a good idea to run the engine when using the windlass to keep the battery charged.*

Preparing the anchor

- Is there sufficient cable on board for the depth? In light to moderate conditions use a ratio of 5:1 length of chain to depth, or 8:1 length of rope to depth.
- Approach the anchorage, check other boats. Are they anchored or moored? Where are their anchors? Are they a similar size to yours?
- Choose the spot to lay anchor, check depth is good, approach the spot slowly into the wind or tide (check how other boats are lying).
- If you have crew, ask someone to operate the anchor at the bow.

Laying anchor

- Stop the boat, lower the anchor under control to the seabed.
- Reverse slowly away, laying out cable in a controlled manner.
- When sufficient cable is let out, select neutral and check that the chain is tight and anchor is set and holding.
- If unsure, use a little reverse thrust to check it is holding.
- Take visual bearings of objects ashore to check the anchor is not dragging. Remember the boat will swing on the anchor.
- Set deep and shallow alarms on the depth sounder. Then relax...

Weighing anchor

- To raise anchor, motor slowly towards it until the chain is vertically above it. Ask a crew member to indicate when, with hand signals.
- Now bring in the chain, keeping it as near vertical as possible.
- If the anchor does not break out, cleat the chain tight and motor gently astern until the anchor breaks out.

COMMUNICATIONS

There are many ways to communicate with others at sea, ranging from signal flags to satellite phones.

Today, leisure sailors are encouraged to use VHF DSC radio as their primary means of communication, since this is both reliable and is monitored by rescue services. Having a basic knowledge of the alternative means and the fundamental principles involved is also helpful and could even prove essential at sea when trying to communicate with other vessels or people ashore. For inshore and coastal sailing, mobile phones are also useful but cannot be relied on as, even when close to the shore, signal is often lost. For blue water cruising sailors, SSB radio is the preferred option.

Every skipper should have a Short Range Certificate, which is compulsory for anyone using a VHF DSC radio. Any crew member who sails regularly is advised to do the one-day course and get their own certificate, so that if for any reason the skipper is unable to use the radio, there are others aboard who know the correct radio procedure and can act quickly if the need arises.

As well as VHF DSC radio operation, this chapter covers up-to-date regulations, the Global Maritime Distress and Safety System (GMDSS), emergency communications equipment and reminders of prowords, the phonetic alphabet, code flags and single letter meanings. It also touches on the Automatic Identification System (AIS) used by merchant shipping, which is also relevant to the leisure sailor.

It is the GMDSS that has enabled DSC (Digital Selective Calling) to be combined with VHF radio to allow users to dial up other vessels by using their unique identity number and have one-to-one conversations rather than broadcasting to all others listening in to a specific VHF channel such as Channel 16. It also permits users to send distress alerts at the touch of a button, which has contributed greatly to safety at sea.

Something to bear in mind is that the International Collision Regulations do not state that one-to-one communications equipment should be used for collision avoidance and it is always best to adhere to the rules and avoid a close-quarters situation.

Understanding the bigger picture of maritime communications helps build confidence when choosing, installing and operating your own equipment, knowing its capabilities and limitations, and ensuring it performs as well as it is designed to. And if your equipment fails, then there are other ways to attract attention and communicate with others, including the use of handheld devices.

Note: Emergency radio procedures are covered later in the book on pages 179–181.

▲ When using a radio, operators should speak clearly at normal conversation level. Emphasise words with weak syllables and familiarise yourself with standard message procedures.

are waterproof and can be very useful in an emergency.

When a VHF DSC radio is turned on it automatically monitors Channel 70 for emergency calls. If another vessel transmits a digital alert then this is picked up by the receiver and causes a high-pitched audio alarm to sound. The position of the vessel in distress and the time of the signal are given in text format. Voice communications can continue on Channel 16 as with a standard VHF radio.

In an emergency, anyone may use a VHF DSC radio to call for help on Channel 16. A VHF DSC radio may be operated by a non-qualified user under the supervision of a qualified operator.

VHF DSC Radio

VHF DSC radio is now the main means of communication at sea, including by the rescue services. The skipper and designated radio operator must be qualified to use the equipment. VHF DSC radios are available as fixed radios attached to a vessel or as handheld personal radios. Fixed radios are generally more powerful and have a better range than handheld radios. The fixed radio's range is greatly improved when its antenna is fixed to the top of a tall mast. Handheld radios are smaller, portable, most

In an Emergency

In an emergency, press the VHF DSC radio's red button for 15 seconds and then transmit a voice message on Channel 16. See pages 179–181 for Emergency Radio Procedures.

DISTRESS

▼ The typical controls of a basic VHF DSC radio include the features shown here. Displays and layout vary according to manufacturer.

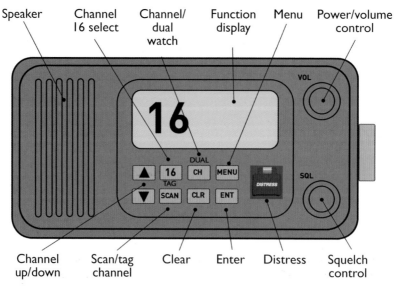

Speaker | Channel 16 select | Channel/dual watch | Function display | Menu | Power/volume control

Channel up/down | Scan/tag channel | Clear | Enter | Distress | Squelch control

If a VHF DSC radio is linked to a GPS then it will automatically include the vessel's position, as well as its identity, when sending a distress alert.

VHF DSC uses Channel 70 for automatic listening. The radio can be tuned to any other channel at the same time.

Advantages of VHF DSC over standard VHF

VHF DSC radio has several important advantages over standard VHF:

- Ability to alert other vessels or rescue centres in an emergency at the press of a red distress button, which sets off audio alarms on all DSC radios within range
- Ability to direct information to specific digital addresses
- Better accuracy of data
- Improved range
- Automatically monitors Channel 70 for distress signals

▼ A VHF DSC radio that is linked to the vessel's GPS shows its position on the display screen. The display includes the current time, plus menu items under consideration such as power level, transmitting indicator and channel scan function.

▲ Handheld VHF radios are ideal for short range use but have low transmitting power and will not perform as well as a fixed radio.

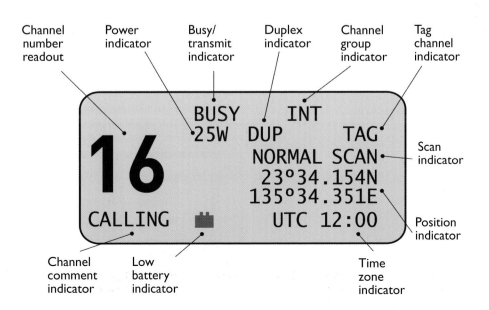

| Channel number readout | Power indicator | Busy/ transmit indicator | Duplex indicator | Channel group indicator | Tag channel indicator |

BUSY   INT
25W DUP   TAG
NORMAL SCAN
23°34.154N
135°34.351E
CALLING   UTC 12:00

Scan indicator

Position indicator

Channel comment indicator

Low battery indicator

Time zone indicator

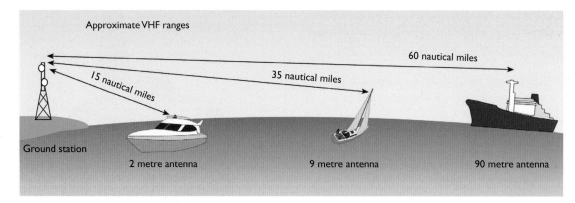

Approximate VHF ranges

60 nautical miles

15 nautical miles

35 nautical miles

Ground station

2 metre antenna

9 metre antenna

90 metre antenna

▲ *VHF radio signals travel in straight lines, so the range of a VHF radio depends very much on the height and quality of its antenna.*

VHF Range

Antenna:
VHF radios operate on line of sight transmission, so their range is very limited in comparison with other forms of communication, such as a satellite phone, for example. There is an advantage for a radio antenna to be sited as high as possible above sea level to get maximum range, so a sailing vessel with an antenna attached to the top of its 20 metre mast will have much better VHF range than a power boat with a 4 metre mast.

Power:
VHF range performance is affected by the power of the radio. High-power settings produce a better quality signal. The downside is that this consumes more battery life. Most VHF radios have high and low settings, which allows battery life conservation.

High power of 25 watts gives a signal extra strength to reach maximum range, but for normal usage one watt will suffice and consume much less power. Portable radios tend to have a limited high power of about 5 watts as they have limited battery size.

A DSC VHF gives up to 20 per cent better performance than an analogue VHF as a digital signal is more efficient than an analogue signal and is more likely to travel to the limit of the radio horizon.

Capture effect:
When a VHF DSC radio is switched on but not

transmitting, it will lock on to the strongest signal being broadcast on the selected channel in the vicinity. This is known as the Capture Effect. For this reason, it is good radio protocol to use low-power settings when making transmissions and only switch to high-power settings if you are making a distress call or communicating with a shore station.

Installation:
The radio set should be well away from the main compass, engine and areas likely to be affected by spray. Check the manufacturer's instructions if in doubt. For short-handed sailing, it is useful to have a cockpit speaker and some manufacturers can supply extension microphone transmitters, which can also be installed in the cockpit or just inside the companionway.

VHF radio licence

In many countries it is a legal requirement for both users and vessels to have VHF licences. For countries outside the UK, you are advised to

▼ *In the UK, the Short Range Certificate is issued by the RYA after successful completion of a one-day course and written test. Online courses are also available.*

check the legal requirements for licences and training locally. Note it is not a legal requirement to hold a VHF licence in the USA.

In the UK, operators are required to obtain a Short Range Certificate (SRC), which covers VHF radio use in the GMDSS A1 sea areas. One-day courses and certification are administered by the Royal Yachting Association: www.rya.org.uk. For radio use outside the GMDSS A1 sea areas, a Long Range Certificate (LRC) is necessary. Courses and certification are administered by AMERC: www.amerc.ac.uk.

MMSI

Maritime Mobile Service Identity (MMSI) numbers are a kind of digital VHF telephone number consisting of 9 digits. When a vessel's DSC radio is licensed it is given a unique MMSI number, which identifies the vessel and its country of registration. The MMSI number is then automatically included with DSC messages. If the operator knows another vessel's MMSI number then they can contact that vessel specifically, unlike with basic VHF radio.

In a similar way to telephone numbers, MMSI numbers for vessels (of all sizes) begin with a three digit national code (eg 232, 233, 234 and 235 for the UK) followed by a six digit individual station (ie vessel) number.

▼ VHF channels are allocated for specific purposes including distress, digital selective calling, inter-ship and shore-based operations.

CHANNEL	PURPOSE
Ch 0	Search and Rescue (SAR) operations, not for pleasure craft.
Ch 6, 8, 72, 77	Ship to ship.
Ch 10	Maritime Safety Information (MSI) broadcasts.
Ch 11, 12, 14	Used for port operations.
Ch 13	Inter-ship communications relating to navigational safety. Can be used by pleasure craft to contact merchant ships if no response on Channel 16.
Ch 16	Distress, safety and calling***.
Ch 67	Small craft safety channels used by UK Coastguard.
Ch 70	Reserved for sending Digital Selective Calling for Distress and Safety under GMDSS.
Ch 80	Used for communication between UK marinas and visiting boats.
Ch M	Secondary working channel.
Ch M2	Used for yacht racing.

*** Channel 16 VHF is the international distress frequency, used for broadcasting distress calls (MAYDAY, Pan-Pan, Securite etc). It is also used for vessels to call up others and shore stations. After contact is made, the call has to be switched to another channel (eg Channel 6, 8, 72, 77) to keep Channel 16 free for emergency use.

▼ VHF DSC radios should be sited in dry surroundings well away from the steering compass. A cockpit repeater speaker is a useful addition, especially for short-handed crews.

SSB radio

Marine SSB (Single Side Band) radio enables worldwide communication and is widely used by blue water cruising yachts. The range of High Frequency (HF) SSB is several thousand miles and is the cheapest form of long range communication at sea. Medium Frequency (MF) works up to 150 nautical miles from the coast. SSB radios are more complex to operate than VHF radios, with many more frequencies and channels. Modern transceivers usually have pre-programmed channels.

The power needed for a SSB radio is more than is required for a VHF, typically using 25 amps when transmitting. The radio antenna needs to be substantial and is often attached to the backstay as an insulated section; in some cases a tall whip antenna is installed. In order to get good radio reception, a bronze ground plate needs to be attached to the outside of plastic hulls (not necessary on steel hulls). Also needed is an antenna coupler, or automatic antenna tuner, which helps tune the radio and antenna together to the selected frequency, saving constant manual adjustment.

SSB radio:

- Operates on shortwave, medium frequency (MF) and high frequency (HF) – 2MHz–26MHz.
- Enables voice communication with other vessels and coastal radio stations while on long offshore passages.
- Enables access to ocean weather data including GRIB files, Weatherfax and NAVTEX.
- Enables email transmission. This requires having a contract with a commercial service such as GlobalMarineNet or to subscribe to user-owned service SailMail.
- Uses Digital Selective Calling (DSC).
- Calls are free.

Radio licences and training

In the UK, SSB radio usage requires two licences:
- a Ship Radio Licence
- a Long Range Certificate (LRC)

Courses and certification are administered by AMERC: www.amerc.ac.uk.
Note: For countries outside the UK, we advise you check the legal requirements for licences and training locally.

 TIP

- Installation of an SSB radio is not straightforward and can result in poor performance if not fitted by an SSB specialist.

▼ *An SSB radio needs a substantial antenna and a ground plate fixed to the hull for it to work efficiently.*

▼ *This yacht is well set up for offshore cruising, with an SSB aerial attached to the backstay plus a whip antenna on the stern.*

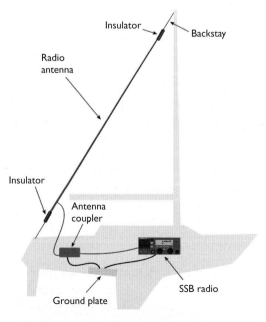

▲ *A satellite phone can easily be mistaken for an old-style regular mobile phone, but is in a completely different class, offering worldwide coverage. Calls are expensive and data transmissions are much higher than landlines.*

Many blue water sailors become amateur radio operators or 'HAMs', which enables them to use amateur radio bands. Getting a HAM certificate can have benefits in terms of operating costs.

Satellite phone

A satellite telephone is similar in appearance and functionality to a mobile phone, but connects to satellites instead of a normal cellular telephone network. You can use satellite telephones at sea where mobile phones are out of range. Satellite phones also use international standard dialling codes and telephone numbers. This means that you can pre-programme the phone contacts menu with the telephone numbers of, for example, the Maritime Rescue Coordination Centres (MRCCs) you might need to contact in an emergency.

Satellite phones can receive emails and are a reliable way to download weather data such as synoptic charts and GRIB files, which can be sent from specialist services and downloaded to a laptop computer. Although satellite phones

are expensive and slow for data downloading, the quality is good and voice reception is usually excellent.

Mobile phone

Mobile phones are not designed to be used at sea, but they can be used close to shore as a means of calling for help if no other means of communication is available. Rescue services do not consider mobile phones to be an effective means of calling for help at sea for a number of reasons:

- They are not waterproof.
- The signal is not guaranteed and there are many black spots.
- Even if your phone is working and has a signal, only one person will hear your call for help.
- The search and rescue agencies cannot pinpoint your position with a mobile phone signal.

 TIPS

- Rescue services strongly recommend the use of VHF DSC marine radios.
- There are many types of waterproof cover available for mobile phones, well worth purchasing.

▲ *A good quality waterproof cover will protect a smartphone. Though mobile reception fades a few miles offshore, apps for smartphones and tablets provide valuable complementary information for sailors and boaters.*

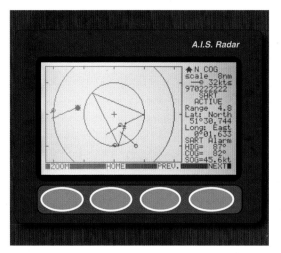

▲ AIS plotters provide the user with detailed information about ships in their vicinity, including the types of vessel, their speed, track and bearing from the user.

AIS

AIS (Automated Identification System) is an international tracking system used to identify and locate commercial vessels at sea. These vessels use a special transceiver that continually broadcasts key data via dedicated VHF channels. AIS is primarily intended as an automatic collision avoidance system.

AIS has become increasingly popular with pleasure vessels as a tool to help with collision avoidance, in addition to traditional methods such as radar and lookout. It is not a legal requirement for pleasure vessels to install AIS, so an option is to install an AIS receiver that connects with the VHF antenna and then displays data on a radar, chart plotter or laptop computer. AIS is now included with many chart plotters, with data overlaid on electronic charts to show all AIS-equipped vessels in your area.

AIS provides the following data:

- GPS position
- Speed
- Course
- Name
- Destination
- Call-sign
- Cargo
- MMSI registration
- Vessel size

GMDSS

The Global Maritime Distress and Safety System (GMDSS) is an internationally agreed system introduced by the International Maritime Organization (IMO) enabling search and rescue authorities, as well as shipping, to be alerted quickly if a vessel is in distress.

GMDSS performs the following:

- Alerts the position of the casualty vessel
- Search and Rescue coordination
- Locates and homes in on the casualty
- Maritime safety information broadcasts
- General communications
- Bridge to bridge communications

GMDSS components include:

- Emergency Position Indicating Radio Beacon (EPIRB)
- NAVTEX
- Inmarsat B, C and F77
- High Frequency radio
- Search and Rescue Radar Transponders (SART)
- Digital Selective Calling

▼ AIS receivers can be connected by USB cables to laptops and tablet devices. For obvious reasons, only vessels transmitting data will show up. To be seen by others it is necessary to fit an AIS transponder.

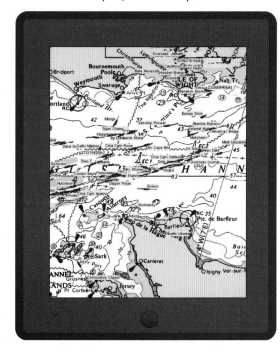

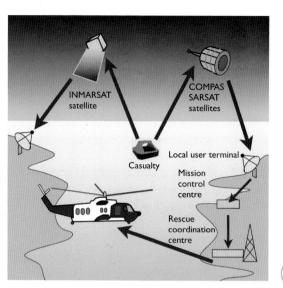

▲ *The primary purpose of the GMDSS is to automate and improve emergency communications for the world's shipping industry.*

GMDSS sea areas

The number and type of radio safety equipment vessels are required to have depends on the sea areas they are navigating in.

Sea Area A1 – Coverage of VHF coast stations (up to 40 miles for a 15m mast).
Sea Area A2 – Coverage of MF coast stations (up to 150 miles).
Sea Area A3 – Coverage of Inmarsat satellites (between 70°N and 70°S).
Sea Area A4 – Polar regions.

Note: Recreational vessels and vessels under 300 tons are not subject to GMDSS regulations.

Inmarsat-C

The Inmarsat-C system is a global maritime distress and tracking service that has become a mainstay of maritime safety and security as part of the Global Maritime Distress Safety System (GMDSS). Inmarsat-C allows you to send and receive high-speed data, email and telephone messages via satellite when you're out of range of land communications.

▶ *Ocean racing fleets carry sophisticated 24/7 satellite systems, providing safety services, vessel tracking, audio and video communications, plus social media access. This enables online audiences to stay in touch with race progress as it happens.*

Inmarsat-C includes:

- Data transfer
- Email
- SMS
- Telex
- Remote monitoring
- Tracking (position reporting)
- Chart and weather updates
- Maritime Safety Information (MSI)
- Maritime security
- GMDSS
- SafetyNET

 TIP

- Inmarsat-C is designed for offshore communications. If you never sail more than 30 nautical miles offshore you do not need this equipment.

NAVTEX and SafetyNET

NAVTEX (short for NAVigational TEXt messages) is a free service that operates internationally and provides weather forecasts, Maritime Safety Information (MSI) including nav warnings and search and rescue information. NAVTEX broadcasts have a minimum range of 250 nautical miles from land, well beyond coastal VHF broadcasts.

NAVTEX is an integral part of the worldwide GMDSS, transmitting routine broadcasts in 10-minute time slots in text format every four hours. Urgent information – distress information, gale warnings – may be broadcast at any time.

NAVAREAS

Transmissions are made from local transmitting stations around the world in 23 Navareas (also known as Metareas). Each station has a call sign ID and set times when it broadcasts.

NAVTEX frequencies

There are two main NAVTEX frequencies. International broadcasts are on 518 kHz in English. Local inshore waters forecasts are broadcast on 490 kHz in local national languages.

▼ *NAVTEX receivers can be programmed to receive data from selected stations and message categories. Transmission schedules can be found in nautical almanacs and on the internet.*

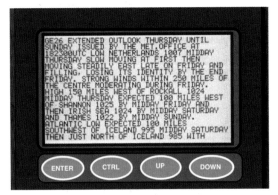

NAVTEX receivers

NAVTEX receivers store the text information they receive. This can then be viewed as a scrollable LCD display or printed on a paper roll, depending on the type of equipment. NAVTEX uses abbreviations to keep weather forecasts and messages short.

NAVTEX can also be accessed on PCs, using special software that connects to a radio that receives the NAVTEX frequencies. This avoids the need to buy dedicated receivers.

Skippers can programme their receivers to filter out information they do not require, such as transmissions from outside their navigation area or those not applicable to small vessels. In the UK, MCA guidance is that all pleasure and other small craft sailing around the coast or going offshore should have NAVTEX.

NAVTEX Messages

NAVTEX messages use the following format:

- 1st character is the code letter of transmitting station.
- 2nd character is message category (see below).
- 3rd and 4th characters are message serial numbers.
- Serial number 00 are urgent messages.
- NAVTEX messages end NNNN.

Message Categories:

A*	Navigational warnings
B*	Meteorological warnings
C	Ice reports
D*	SAR information and piracy attack warnings
E	Weather forecasts
F	Pilot service
G	AIS
H	LORAN
I	Spare
J	SATNAV
K	Other electronic Navaids
L	Navwarnings additional to A
M–U	Spare
V–Y	Special services – as allocated
Z	No messages on hand

*These categories cannot be deselected by the receiver.

SafetyNET

Inmarsat-C SafetyNET is an internationally adopted, automated satellite system providing

NAVTEX Abbreviations

Metres	M	Rapidly	RPDY
Meteo...	MET	Scattered	SCT
Moderate	MOD	Severe	SEV/SVR
Moving/Move	MOV or MVG	Showers	SHWRS/SH
No change	NC	Significant	SIG
Nautical miles	NM	Slight	SLGT or SLT
No significant change	NOSIG	Slowly	SLWY
Next	NXT	Stationary	STNR
Occasionally	OCNL	Strong	STRG
Occlusion Front	O-FRONT/ OFNT	Temporarily/ Temporary	TEMPO
Possible	POSS	Further outlooks	TEND
Probability/ Probable	PROB	Veering	VEER
Quickly	QCKY	Visibility	VIS
Quasi-stationary	QSTNR	Variable	VRB
Quadrant	QUAD	Warm front	W-FRONT/WFNT

NAVTEX Abbreviations

North (erly)	N	Forecast	FCST
Northeast (erly)	NE	Filling	FLN
East (erly)	E	Following	FLW
Southeast (erly)	SE	From	FM
South (erly)	SE	Frequent/ Frequency	FRQ
Southwest (erly)	SW	HectoPascal	HPA
West (erly)	W	Heavy	HVY
Northwest (erly)	NW	Improving/Improve	IMPR
Backing	BACK	Increasing	INCR
Becoming	BECMG	Intensifying/ Intensify	INTSF
Building	BLDN	Isolated	ISOL
Cold Front	C-FRONT/CFNT	Km/h	KMH
Decreasing	DECR	Knots	KT
Deepening	DPN	Latitude/ Longitude	LAT/LONG
Expected	EXP	Locally	LOC

▲ *NAVTEX messages use an internationally agreed list of abbreviations for commonly used words to shorten the texts broadcast.*

weather forecasts and warnings, marine navigational warnings and other safety related information to all types of vessels around the world. SafetyNET is part of the Global Maritime Distress and Safety System (GMDSS) and is recognised as being one of the primary means for broadcasting and automatic reception of maritime safety information (MSI), along with NAVTEX.

SafetyNET uses a system called Enhanced Group Call (EGC), which also supports FleetNET, another service for ships. Merchant ships are required by law to carry equipment capable of receiving and broadcasting the SafetyNET service. Blue water cruising and racing sailors are not required to carry such equipment but often do so. Race organisers often require this as a condition of entry.

SafetyNET provides urgency messages and navigational warnings; coastal warnings; shore-to-ship distress alerts; search-and-rescue coordination messages; meteorological and navigational warnings and meteorological forecasts.

MSI is defined by the International Maritime Organization as: 'Navigational and meteorological warnings, meteorological forecasts, and other urgent safety-related messages broadcast to ships.' MSI providers include national meteorological services, which supply weather data; hydrographic offices, which supply navigation warnings and chart correction data; rescue co-ordination centres, for shore-to-ship distress alerts and Search and Rescue (SAR) coordination; and The International Ice Patrol, for North Atlantic ice hazards.

SafetyNET messages include a special header consisting of five 'C' codes:
C0 – ocean area code.
C1 – priority code – 1 digit – distress, urgency, safety, routine.
C2 – service code – 2 digits – type of message broadcast.
C3 – address code – 12 characters – area broadcast instructions.
C4 – repetition rate – 2 digits – number and frequency of broadcasts.
C5 – presentation code – 2 digits – type of alphabet used.

EPIRB

Emergency Position Indicating Radio Beacons (EPIRBs) transmit distress signals via the COSPAS/SARSAT satellite system and earth stations to search and rescue (SAR) services. EPIRBs use a frequency of 406MHz, which enables reliable and strong transmission to satellites.

EPIRBs are installed on boats and can be operated either manually or automatically when submerged in water, using a hydrostatic release system. EPIRBs have to be fitted on commercial shipping by law but are not compulsory on private vessels.

Key facts:

- Global coverage
- Registration enables SAR authorities to identify casualty vessel and launch appropriate rescue teams
- 406MHz transmission to COSPAS/SARSAT satellites
- 121.5MHz homing frequency
- Built-in GPS enables pinpoint accuracy
- Built-in flashing lights aid nighttime recovery
- Battery life minimum 48 hours

▼ EPIRBS are waterproof and buoyant. Once activated, rescue services are alerted within a few minutes of the transmitter's position, which is updated every 20 minutes. Accuracy can be within 100 metres or less. They need a clear view skywards to work effectively.

Each EPIRB unit has a unique digital identity number, which identifies the vessel and its details, allowing rescue services to eliminate false alerts and launch appropriate rescues. Most EPIRBs are equipped with integral GPS, which provides pinpoint accuracy of a casualty vessel's location. Units without inbuilt GPS make location of the casualty more difficult as their position is calculated by Low Earth Orbit satellites, which are not as fast and accurate as GPS. In addition to the 406MHz signal, most EPIRBs transmit a homing signal on 121.5MHz, which enables rescue services to home in on the casualty.

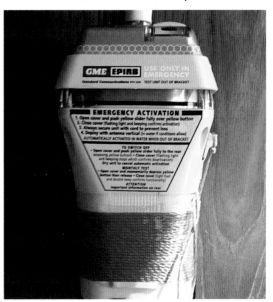

▲ EPIRBs are self-contained, battery operated radio transmitters and intended for emergency use only. Note the line, which can be tied to a liferaft.

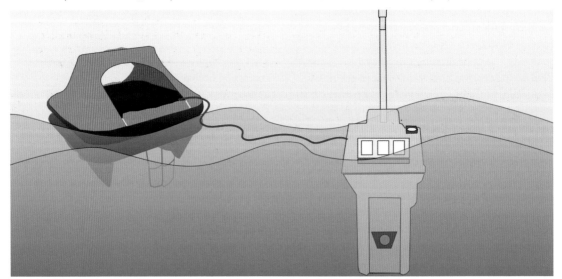

Personal Locator Beacon

Personal Locator Beacons (PLBs) are small dedicated devices that transmit distress signals via satellite to search and rescue (SAR) services. PLBs use a frequency of 406MHz, the same frequency used by EPIRBs (Emergency Position Indicating Radio Beacons).

Each PLB has a unique 15 digit identity number, which identifies the user and their personal details, plus emergency contacts for rescue services to call. These details are transmitted with the distress signal via the COSPAS/SARSAT satellite system to the SAR centre in the country where the device is registered.

PLBs equipped with integral GPS provide pinpoint accuracy of a casualty's location. Units without inbuilt GPS make location of the casualty more difficult as their position is calculated by Low Earth Orbit satellites, which are not as fast and accurate as GPS.

In addition to the 406MHz signal, PLBs transmit a homing signal on 121.5MHz, which enables rescuers to home in on the casualty.

Key facts:

- Global coverage
- PLBs are registered to enable SAR authorities to notify emergency contacts and speed up rescue efforts
- 406MHz transmission to COSPAS/SARSAT satellites
- 121.5MHz homing frequency
- Built-in GPS best as enables pinpoint accuracy
- Built-in flashing lights aid nighttime recovery
- Battery life of 24–48 hours
- Waterproof

MOB beacons

MOB (Man Overboard) beacons are short range PLB transmitters designed to be worn by crew members of yachts and other small vessels. They use the 121.5MHz frequency and transmit distress signals to receivers installed in the parent craft.

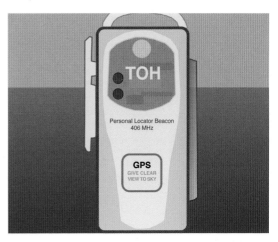

▲ Personal Locator Beacons transmit for a minimum of 24 hours and have inbuilt GPS, which pinpoints their location and is used to alert the nearest rescue centre.

SART

A Search and Rescue Transponder (SART) is used as a homing device to help rescue craft locate a liferaft or casualty vessel. A SART performs best when at least 1 metre above sea level so needs to be attached to a liferaft on a pole. It will then have a range of about 5 nautical miles from a rescue vessel's radar or up to 40 miles from an aircraft.

SARTs work by reacting to X-Band 3cm radar transmissions, sending a series of pulses, which are picked up by the rescue vessel's radar.

▼ A SART responds to a radar pulse sent from a rescue vessel and transmits a response, which shows up as a series of dots on the rescue vessel's radar. As the rescue vessel gets closer, the radar screen shows concentric circles.

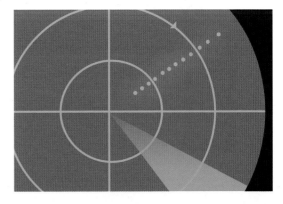

Single letter meanings

A		I have a diver down; keep well clear at slow speed.
B		I am taking in, or discharging, or carrying dangerous goods.
C		Yes.
D		Keep clear of me; I am manoeuvring with difficulty.
E		I am altering course to starboard.
F		I am disabled; communicate with me.
G		I require a pilot. When made by fishing boats 'I am hauling in my nets'.
H		I have a pilot on board.
I		I am altering my course to port.
J		I am on fire and have dangerous cargo; keep well clear of me.
K		I wish to communicate with you.
L		You should stop your vessel instantly.
M		My vessel is stopped and making no way through the water.
N		No.
O		Man overboard.
P		Vessel about to put to sea. By fishing vessels 'My nets are caught fast'.
Q		My vessel is 'healthy' and I request free pratique.
R		The way is off my ship.
S		My engines are going astern.
T		Keep clear of me; I am engaged in pair trawling.
U		You are running into danger.
V		I require assistance.
W		I require medical assistance.
X		Stop carrying out your intentions and watch for my signals.
Y		I am dragging my anchor.
Z		I require a tug. By fishing vessels 'I am shooting nets'.

▲ Single-letter signals overcome language barriers and communicate urgent, important and common messages quickly and effectively.

Phonetic Alphabet

A	alpha	B	bravo
C	charlie	D	delta
E	echo	F	foxtrot
G	golf	H	hotel
I	india	J	juliet
K	kilo	L	lima
M	mike	N	november
O	oscar	P	papa
Q	quebec	R	romeo
S	sierra	T	tango
U	uniform	V	victor
W	whiskey	X	x-ray
Y	yankee	Z	zulu

▲ It is a good idea to display your vessel's callsign spelt phonetically alongside the radio.

Prowords

Prowords, or Procedural Words, are used to help keep radio communications clear, concise and easy to understand.

▼ Prowords are worth memorising and are used to avoid confusion or misunderstanding when communicating by radio.

PROWORD	EXPLANATION
CALL SIGN	The group that follows is a call sign.
CORRECT	You are correct, or what you have transmitted is correct.
CORRECTION	I am correcting the last part of my message.
FIGURES	Numbers or numerals to follow.
I SAY AGAIN	I am repeating transmission or portion indicated.
I SPELL	I shall spell the next word phonetically.
OUT	This is the end of my transmission to you and no answer is required or expected.
OVER	This is the end of my transmission to you and a response is necessary. Go ahead, transmit.
ROGER	I have received your last transmission satisfactorily.
SAY AGAIN	Repeat all of your last transmission.
THIS IS	This transmission is from the station whose designator immediately follows.

International Code of Signals

The International Code of Signals (ICS) provides the basis for all vessels at sea to communicate important messages regarding the safety of navigation and persons, especially where there are language difficulties. The ICS is designed for all methods of signalling including flags, flashing lights, sound, voice, radio and even Morse signalling by hand flags or arms.

The ICS allows standardised coded messages to be sent that mean the same in nine languages (English, French, German, Greek, Italian, Japanese, Norwegian, Russian and Spanish).

Signals are arranged in three groups:

- Single-letter signals, which are very urgent, important or common.
- Two-letter signals, which are general messages.
- Three-letter signals beginning with 'M' in the Medical Section.

The Code follows the basic principle that each signal should have a complete meaning. In certain cases "complements" are used to supplement the signal to provide specific or detailed information when either requesting or sending information. For example, the two letter 'IN' = 'I require a diver' can be supplemented to 'IN I' = 'I require a diver to clear propeller'.

It is recommended that all leisure vessels heading offshore carry a copy of The International Code of Signals, which is free to download from the internet. This could prove to be invaluable in an emergency situation, especially if all electrics have failed.

▼ *The International Code of Signals works not only across languages but also for all methods of signalling, old and new.*

▲ *The flags I, N, I are an example of a two letter message plus complement, meaning 'I require a diver to clear propeller'.*

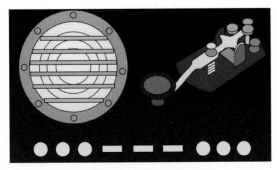

Area of Operation from Coast (Nautical Miles)	Up to 5 NM	Up to 30 NM	Up to 60 NM	Up to 150 NM	>150 NM
Hand-held waterproofed VHF radio – also for use in liferaft	R	R	R	R	R
VHF fixed radio installation – fitted with DSC	O	R	R	R	R
406 MHz float-free EPIRB (with 121.5 MHz homer)	O	O	O	R	R
MF SSB radio installation – fitted with DSC	None	None	O	R	R
INMARSAT	None	None	O	O	R
NAVTEX receiver – useable up to ~ 400 NM from coast	None	O	R	R	R
Search and Rescue Transponder (SART)	None	O	O	R	R

▲ *MCA Recommendations for leisure vessels*
R=Recommended   O=Optional

4 EQUIPMENT AND MAINTENANCE

The best skippers learn how to maintain and conserve equipment, how to avoid and identify potential problems and how to cope when things go wrong.

Those of us who enjoy going sailing don't necessarily enjoy working on engines and there are some famous examples of sailing legends such as Don Street who removed the engine from his yawl *Iolaire* to make space below decks for a much more useful thing in his opinion, his writing desk. Arguably, we should not have to rely on engines to remain safe and likewise we should not have to rely on other sophisticated electronic equipment either. However, it does make sense for skippers to understand as thoroughly as possible all the various systems that are found aboard a modern yacht, how to service them and how to troubleshoot and repair them if they fail.

This chapter is full of useful tips on engine maintenance, fuel systems, cooling systems, electrics, instruments, water systems, plus essential spares and tools to carry on board. There is plenty of advice on common problems, fault finding and the importance of having backup equipment if your primary equipment fails. There is also detailed advice on safety and emergency equipment, from lifejackets to liferafts, with emphasis placed on the need to keep safety equipment properly maintained and to replace it when it is out of date. Equally important is to equip your boat with the basics, such as efficient radar reflectors, paper charts, well-maintained batteries and plenty of fresh water.

The ability to be as self sufficient as possible when at sea is very important, but at the same time loading a boat with unnecessary amounts of gear for short trips can add considerable weight and cause problems in rough weather when things start flying around.

Learning how to be efficient is key, as is understanding that a lot of boating is about compromise. If you want to sail the fastest boat on the water, then you have to give up the luxuries and concentrate on reducing weight in order to make your boat as efficient as possible. If you want comfort and all the mod cons then you are more likely to end up with a slower and more cumbersome boat, but one that you can happily live aboard securely for long periods of time. If you want to be able to combine speed and comfort, then the cost factor will most likely become significant. In the end, when equipping your boat much comes down to common sense, as to a large extent it depends on whether you plan to sail for long periods offshore or to restrict your activity to day sailing inshore.

Engine maintenance, filters and spares

Looking after the engine is one of the key factors in reducing the potential for unnecessary drama on board any boat. The base units of marine engines are normally very robust – most are based on industrial units designed to run 24 hours a day for years at a time, or are adapted from truck engines that are similarly expected to run for a million miles or more. However, it's not unknown for an abused engine to die prematurely and it will certainly be less reliable than one that's well cared for.

At a basic level, all that a simple diesel engine of up to around 50hp – the type typically installed in a sailing yacht – needs to run is a supply of clean fuel and air, plus a functioning cooling system. Electrical power is often needed only for starting, although even some relatively basic engines have an electrical solenoid fuel shut-off switch that uses a small amount of power to keep it open while the engine is running. However, more sophisticated engines, such as recent models

▼ Dirty fuel has the potential to quickly block filters, especially in rough seas.

▲ Engine failure is by far the biggest single reason for lifeboat rescues.

producing several hundred horsepower that drive larger motor yachts, will have much more complicated electronic systems.

In the marine environment many engine problems stem from lack of use, rather than overuse, and it's a fallacy to think that, because your engine has had only a few tens of hours of use over a 12-month period since its last service, it's not due for another.

Diesel bug

Low use means fuel may remain in the tank for months or even years at a time, giving plenty of time for bacteria to grow that will be certain to block fuel filters eventually. This feeds at the interface of the fuel and any water in the tank and on the (roughly 10 per cent) ethanol content of most modern fuels. Bacteria can be kept at bay by ensuring tanks are kept topped up, especially over winter, so that condensation can't form on the internal walls, and by using a proprietary anti-bacterial product. It's also worth cleaning the tank every few seasons and immediately after buying a second-hand boat if there's any doubt about the maintenance history.

Daily checks

Maintenance is the key to reliability. As well as servicing annually (or more often if specified by the manufacturer), a quick daily check will often identify problems before they cause a breakdown. A big part of looking after an engine is noticing small changes that are hints of impending problems, such as an increase of black dust around drive belts, which show they are wearing rapidly, or a gradual increase in oil consumption.

Before starting:

- General look at condition of hoses and wiring
- Check for fluid leaks – oil, fuel, water
- Alternator and water pump drive belt tension and condition
- Engine oil level
- Gearbox oil level
- Cooling water level (indirect cooled engines)
- Fuel system water separator
- Cooling water seacock open
- Raw water strainer
- Correct operation of alarms and warning lights
- If the engine is run for more than 8 hours, the motor should be stopped and the items above checked again

▼ Check the operation of warning lights and alarms as part of your daily checks.

As soon as the engine starts:

- Oil pressure
- Charging voltage
- Flow of cooling water from exhaust
- Fuel level should be monitored throughout any voyage, allowing for a 20 per cent reserve

▲ Daily checks help you get to know your engine and minimise the chance of failure.

 **TIP**

Know your engine

Ideally you should be able to identify and locate the following items on your engine and its installation:

- Fuel filters and water separator
- Bleed screw(s) on engine-mounted fuel filter and injector pump
- Fuel lift pump
- Raw water pump impeller
- Drive belts for alternator and water pump(s)
- Cooling water intake skin fitting and filter
- Engine start battery
- Domestic batteries
- Whether the engine is directly cooled by seawater pumped around the motor, or whether it's indirectly cooled
- Heat exchanger and header tank (if engine is indirectly cooled)
- Whether a turbocharger is fitted

Routine servicing

One of the best ways to get to know your engine is by carrying out your own servicing – with a simple engine it will take less than an hour. It is advisable to complete a short diesel engine maintenance course before doing so.

If you don't already have one, it's worth sourcing a workshop and service manual for your engine. However, even the most basic operator's manual will detail service schedules. Typical tasks, in addition to the daily checks, include changing engine oil and oil filters, as well as fuel filters and the water pump impeller and inspecting the condition of the air filter. Once you become familiar with all these procedures, changing fuel filters and bleeding air out of the fuel system or replacing a burnt-out water pump impeller at sea should not present any difficulties.

Routine services are often specified after every 250 hours or 12 months, whichever comes earlier, although in some cases fuel filter changes may be specified as frequently as every 50 hours. However, this figure may be extended by fitting a higher capacity pre-filter in addition to the small one mounted on the engine itself. Every 500 or 1,000 hours more major services are likely to be specified, including replacing the gearbox oil and checking valve clearances.

▼ *The calibration of most tank gauges is notoriously vague – a dipstick is the only way to be sure of the fuel level.*

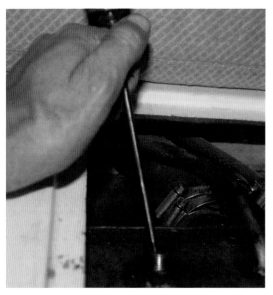

▲ *A combined pre-filter and water separator. The filter should be changed at every service and the bowl checked for evidence of water daily.*

Troubleshooting

When diagnosing problems it's all too easy to jump to conclusions and in doing so miss what should be an obvious problem. It's therefore vital to keep an open mind and work through a methodical process, no matter how urgent the situation appears to be. Irrespective of the problem, the first stage is to spend a minute taking a careful look over the engine, looking for obvious problems such as fluid leaks and loose or broken drive belts.

An engine failure is often the result of several overlapping problems. Therefore, although it may be possible to get it running to get you home by solving a single issue, it's also important to make sure all underlying problems are solved. If not, you can be sure they will return and the future reliability of the engine won't be assured.

▲ *The better your engine access, the easier it is to look after the unit and to solve problems when they occur.*

Essential spares

Be sure to carry the following spares at least:

- Engine oil
- Gearbox oil
- Antifreeze (for indirect cooled engines)
- Drive belts for alternator and water pumps
- Primary and secondary fuel filters
- Water pump impellers
- Hose clips
- Cable ties
- Electrical tape
- Duct tape
- Instant gasket
- Fuses

Boats voyaging longer distances, or operating in remote areas, will want to at least double up on the above items and also include spare hoses for the cooling system.

Essential tools

A basic toolkit and supply of spares is essential for fixing engine problems. Always buy the best tools you can afford – cheap items are liable to round the corners off nuts and so on, which only adds to long-term costs. The following is a minimum:

- Open and ring spanners
- Socket set
- Screwdrivers (selection of both flat and cross-head)
- Pliers
- Molegrips
- Small hack-saw
- Knife
- Wire cutter/crimper
- Large adjustable wrench
- Digital multimeter

Fuel system, air supply and oil pressure

Clean fuel is fundamental to the running of a diesel engine – microscopic dirt particles and water will damage the precision parts in the high-pressure injection pump and even air in the fuel supply will cause the engine to lose power, or stop completely.

Fuel system

The components of the fuel system are a fuel tank, pre-filter and water separator, low-pressure lift pump, fine (engine-mounted) filter, high-pressure injection pump and injectors. The two fuel filters are the primary defence against dirt in the fuel. The pre-filter is normally mounted on a bulkhead and is usually combined with a water separator in the form of a glass bowl underneath the filter.

Any small amounts of water in the fuel will collect at the bottom of the bowl, where it can be seen as a cloudy and opaque layer. A drain plug at the bottom of the separator allows any water to be drained off by loosening the plug a few turns and allowing the water to drip out into a suitable small container.

▲ *Activating the lever below the (low pressure) lift pump to bleed air out of the fuel system.*

Air supply

This is something that is often overlooked, but an engine consumes a far greater volume of air than fuel. If the air intake is restricted, or the air filter dirty, the engine will not perform at its best and may belch out black smoke, indicating unburnt fuel in the exhaust. On the small diesel engines fitted to yachts, lack of air is rarely a serious problem, but it's worth considering if the engine is not running as it should. Larger motor yachts often have forced ventilation systems to ensure sufficient air is delivered to the engines.

Oil pressure

Adequate oil pressure is vital for the correct lubrication of the engine. Even a small drop in

▼ *Basic elements of the fuel system needed to deliver clean diesel to the high pressure injector pump.*

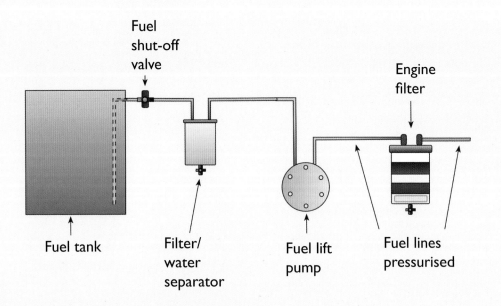

Fuel shut-off valve

Engine filter

Fuel tank

Filter/ water separator

Fuel lift pump

Fuel lines pressurised

pressure can reduce the engine's lifespan, while a major drop may cause significant damage in only a few hours, or minutes, that will require a major rebuild to rectify.

There are three key elements in creating oil pressure. The most obvious is a correctly functioning oil pump – fortunately these tend to be very robust and can be expected to outlast even the most heavily used marine engines. By contrast, engine oil does not have an infinite life – it degrades with both engine use and over time, even if the motor is not used.

Old oil is therefore the most common source of low oil pressure. Second to this is oil of an inappropriate grade – this is often a problem with the motor of older sailing yachts, which tend to be quite primitive, with large tolerances between components, which in turn means modern synthetic oils are not compatible.

It's also important to change oil filters at the manufacturer's recommended intervals, as a partially blocked filter will impact oil pressure. A final aspect of obtaining good oil pressure is the condition of the crankshaft bearings – if these are badly worn, low oil pressure is inevitable. The solution is to remove the crankshaft, replace the bearings and, if necessary, re-grind the shaft.

▲ *Don't overlook an engine's appetite for air – they use a huge amount, particularly when running at high revs.*

▼ *Using a spanner to loosen the bleed screw on the engine-mounted fuel filter assembly.*

▼ *Oil leaks at either end of the crankshaft are normally the result of wear in the main bearings – budget for some expensive repairs if your engine has this problem.*

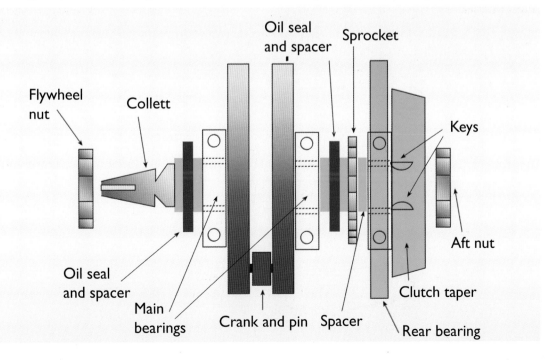

Flywheel nut

Collett

Oil seal and spacer

Sprocket

Keys

Aft nut

Oil seal and spacer

Main bearings

Crank and pin

Spacer

Clutch taper

Rear bearing

The cooling system

There are two main types of cooling system fitted to marine diesel engines, both of which ultimately use seawater for cooling. With the simplest, direct seawater cooling, seawater is pumped around the engine to cool it and then emitted via the exhaust. Indirect cooling systems are more sophisticated, with the coolant in the engine in a closed system, as with the cooling system of a car. Seawater is pumped through a heat exchanger, which cools the fresh water/antifreeze mix in the engine's closed cooling system – in effect the heat exchanger performs the role of a car's radiator.

A third option, usually popular only on vessels built for inland waterways, is termed 'keel cooling'. This is an entirely closed system containing only fresh water and antifreeze, which is pumped through pipework outside the hull below the waterline. It tends to be very reliable, providing the external pipework is not in a location vulnerable to impact damage, as no seawater pump is needed.

▼ *A simple raw water cooling system pumps sea water directly through the engine. This avoids use of a heat exchanger but is not ideal as it increases the risk of corrosion.*

The thermostat keeps the engine at the correct operating temperature. When the engine is cold it limits water flow to the cylinder head only, which allows the engine to warm up quickly. Once the engine is at its normal operating temperature, the thermostat opens to allow water to flow around the main engine block. If the thermostat fails to open then the engine will run too hot. If this is the case it can be removed as a 'get you home' measure – the engine may run cool (which in the long term will increase engine wear) but this is better than it running hot. Anodes are service items that are often forgotten – they prevent corrosion of a direct seawater cooled engine due to hot salt water being pumped around it.

Heat exchangers in indirectly cooled engines are not a 'fit and forget' item – they require periodic attention to check that the relatively narrow waterways are not becoming caked up with calcium deposits.

Cooling system components

The essential components of a direct seawater cooled system are a filter, which prevents debris in the water reaching the engine, an impeller pump, a thermostat and one or two anodes.

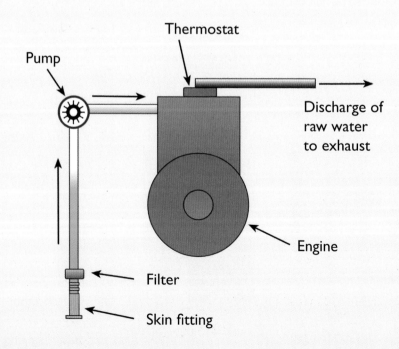

Thermostat

Pump

Discharge of raw water to exhaust

Engine

Filter

Skin fitting

▲ *Cleaning the raw (salt) water filter in the cooling system.*

The seawater side of an indirect cooled system also has the filter and flexible impeller pump of the direct cooling system. In addition, the closed fresh-water/antifreeze system has the thermostat and another water pump. Any problems with a well-maintained engine are most likely in the seawater part of the system.

Engine electrics

We depend on electrics to start the engine and for charging of domestic battery banks to run the vessel's other systems. A failure of the charging system therefore poses the risk of eventually not being able to start the engine and of failure of navigation and domestic systems.

▼ *An indirect cooling system via a heat exchanger allows fresh water/antifreeze to be pumped around the engine, extending its life.*

▲ *Removing the faceplate of a water pump impeller.*

Common problems include loose or badly corroded contacts that block the flow of charge. These should be examined at frequent intervals and, if problems are found, the terminal dismantled, the contacts cleaned thoroughly and then re-assembled. A proactive approach such as this will ensure a higher level of reliability, particularly in boats where wiring is run directly above a damp bilge. It's also worth periodically checking the security of battery terminals as they may become loose over time or even fractured. The electrical system is covered in more detail on pages 102–109.

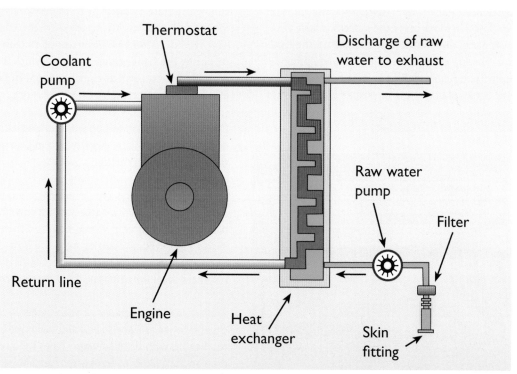

Thermostat

Discharge of raw water to exhaust

Coolant pump

Raw water pump

Filter

Return line

Engine

Heat exchanger

Skin fitting

Electrics

While we depend increasingly on the convenience of a wide variety of on-board electrical systems, water and electricity don't always mix well. Problems are also often exacerbated by the poor standard of wiring in many yachts, particularly older models.

Essential electrics

Failure of any one of the many components of a boat's electrical system could leave you at sea without navigation lights, VHF or the ability to start the engine. Yet boat electrical systems are often neglected, with some crews appearing to put almost blind faith in them, so perhaps it's not surprising that problems are common, especially with older yachts.

It's therefore important for all skippers to have a basic knowledge of boat electrics, both to avoid encountering problems in the first place and to have a chance of solving them at sea without drama. The key principles are easy to grasp and to remember, even for those with little or no existing electrical knowledge.

Most yachts have a 12-volt DC (direct current) system, although larger vessels will have 24-volt electrics. In most cases the system is split into two parts, one for starting the engine, the other for running all the other electrical equipment on board. All boats should have two batteries (or banks of batteries) to ensure there's always

▲ Even small amounts of corrosion on battery terminals can result in a lot of power lost as heat. Make sure they are kept clean.

a well-charged battery for starting the engine that's never used for anything else. In some cases there will also be a third system, with another dedicated battery (or bank of batteries) for powering high current equipment such as electric windlasses, bow thrusters and electric winches.

Batteries

An automotive-type battery, of a similar specification to those used in cars, can be used to supply the starter motor with the very high loads for the few seconds it takes to start the engine. This type of battery, however, is not suitable for powering the boat's other systems, which will typically draw a relatively small amount of power for many hours, or even days, at a stretch.

Deep-discharge (or traction) batteries are designed for slow discharge over a period of time, before being recharged when the engine is running or via shorepower chargers, or solar or wind generators. This type of use would quickly destroy an automotive battery, but a good leisure battery will withstand several hundred such cycles. However, discharging even the best deep-discharge batteries below 50 per cent of their rated capacity will dramatically shorten their life.

There are various grades of such battery – the cheaper ones are not sealed and will need topping up with distilled water from time to time and are likely to have a shorter lifespan

▼ Batteries must be tightly secured to prevent movement in any direction (including vertical).

Two batteries with isolator

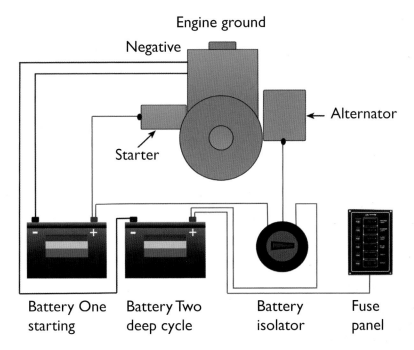

Engine ground

Negative

Starter

Alternator

Battery One
starting

Battery Two
deep cycle

Battery
isolator

Fuse
panel

▲ A separate dedicated battery for engine starting means it will never run flat through powered lights, instruments, heaters and other systems.

than more expensive models. Gel and AGM type batteries cannot spill battery acid and don't produce potentially explosive hydrogen gas when charging. They can withstand many more charge-discharge cycles than conventional deep discharge batteries and so have many advantages for use on boats, despite their higher initial purchase price. Some are also capable of being used for both starting and deep cycling applications.

All batteries lose some of their charge over time – if storing them, for instance over the winter, ensure they are fully charged at the start of the storage period and, if possible, charge once a month to maintain the charge level. Modern three-stage and four-stage mains powered chargers may be left connected permanently. A small solar panel will similarly keep the batteries of boats kept on swinging moorings, and therefore without a source of mains electricity, topped up.

▶ A small solar panel is an easy way to keep batteries topped up when the boat is not being used, but larger panels need to charge via a regulator to prevent battery damage.

Determining battery capacity

Undersized battery banks are one of the key factors behind power failure at sea, as well as the premature failure of (expensive) batteries. It's therefore worth analysing the set-up on your boat to see whether it measures up to the use you give it.

Deep discharge batteries are rated in Amp-hours – a fully charged 100Ah battery, for instance, will deliver 5A for 20 hours before becoming completely discharged. However, discharging even the best deep discharge batteries below 50 per cent of their rated capacity will dramatically shorten their life.

Calculating your estimated daily power usage, by multiplying the current in Amps of each device by the length of time for which you expect to use it, will help determine the size of the batteries needed for the boat. If you aim to charge once a day and don't plan to discharge the batteries to more than 50 per cent of their total capacity, your battery bank should in theory be at least twice the size of your estimated daily power usage.

However, even with good battery charging technologies it becomes increasingly difficult to cram the last 20 per cent of charge into a battery. It's therefore best to size battery banks at around three times the expected daily power usage. Even then, this gives little scope for adding new power-hungry devices such as a fridge or electric autopilot and even with correctly sized batteries it's important to maintain a watch over the battery state throughout a voyage.

Examples of power usage

- Navigation light 1A (boats up to 12m)
- Navigation light 2.5A (boats over 12m)
- Interior lights (each) 1A
- LED lights (each) 0.2A
- Laptop 3–6A
- Instruments 1A
- Chart plotter 1–2A
- Stereo 1–3A
- Auto pilot 3–6A
- Fridge 4A

▲ *Updating charging systems, and keeping them in good order, will pay dividends.*

Looking after the batteries

A corollary to selecting an optimally sized battery bank is that it must also be kept properly charged. With a set of decent batteries costing a minimum of several hundred pounds, it's worth keeping them in optimum condition and never allowing them to discharge below 50 per cent of total charge.

Optimising charging systems will also help to keep batteries topped up to a higher level of charge. The output of standard alternators can drop to as little as one-third of the alternator's rated output after only 15 minutes or so of engine running. However, a smart charging regulator will keep the charging rate close to the initial figure, thus recharging the batteries in minimum time. These have a further advantage in that they charge batteries to as much as 95 per cent of capacity – compared to less than 80 per cent for a standard alternator regulator.

▼ *Changing to LED lighting can significantly reduce power requirements – replacing interior light bulbs is one of the most cost-effective modifications you can make.*

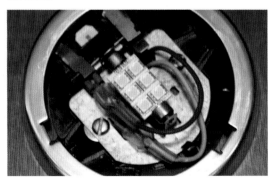

▲ Check the power consumption of your instruments – a boat with multiple displays can use more power than you might expect.

▲ Chart plotters and multifunction displays can use a lot of power – the best can easily be switched to standby mode.

In addition to improving charging systems, minimising the power drawn from batteries will also extend their lifespan. This need not involve major inconveniences – changing to LED lighting, for instance, will significantly reduce daily current drain, and costs significantly less than replacing a battery bank that prematurely runs out of puff. It's also worth ensuring the fridge has at least 4 inches (10cm) of insulation all round. Unfortunately, many are lacking in this respect, which can put a huge strain on batteries.

▼ It is a good idea to make a list of your boat's daily power usage and see how this compares with your batteries' capacities in order to prevent them discharging below 50 per cent of their total charge.

▲ Don't underestimate the power requirements of a laptop, especially if it's connected to the internet via a 3G or 4G mobile dongle.

Item	power draw	hours used	daily amp hours
Nav/anchor lights	1A	8	8Ah / day
LED interior lights	1A	4	4Ah / day
Fridge	1.5A	14	36Ah / day
Instruments	1A	15	15Ah / day
MFD/chartplotter	2.2A	15	16Ah / day
Water pumps	8A	1.5	12Ah / day
Laptop charger	5A	3	15Ah / day
Smartphone charger	0.7A	12	8.4Ah / day
Total daily use			115Ah

Avoiding and identifying electrical problems

The diagnosis of many electrical problems afloat is within the grasp of anyone with basic knowledge of electrical systems and a few key skills.

Battery state

At a basic level, one of the most useful diagnostic tools is a simple digital voltmeter. The voltage produced by a battery, when no load is being drawn from it, is a good guide to its state of charge. When fully charged, a 12V battery can theoretically hold up to 13.2V, although in practice 12.8V or 12.9V is a more likely maximum. At 12.5V, the battery has 75 per cent of its maximum charge remaining, and at 12.2V there's 50 per cent of the battery's total capacity left – the point at which the battery should be recharged.

If the reading drops to 12.0V, there's only 20 per cent of the battery's capacity remaining, and the battery will be (almost) fully discharged at

▼ *The no-load reading of 12.83 volts on this battery indicates it's almost fully charged.*

11.8V. A battery that's nearing the end of its life may still give reasonable voltage readings when fully charged, but only if no load is being drawn. Switching a couple of lights on will create a large voltage drop in a weak battery, whereas an example in good condition will show a drop of only 0.1 or 0.2V in these conditions.

The voltmeter can also be used to check that the alternator is producing charge. Standard alternators have their output capped at around 14.2–14.4V, although there may be a voltage drop of 0.5V, and occasionally more, by the time the charge reaches the batteries. If there is little or no increase in voltage across the battery when the engine is running, then it's very likely that there's a problem with the charging system that will need further investigation.

Battery monitors

Unfortunately, it takes a long time for battery voltages to settle when load is removed, or after charging, and while a reasonably stable voltage may be seen after a few minutes, it takes several hours for the voltage to completely stabilise. This is one of the benefits of more sophisticated battery monitors, which give a precise indication at any time of how much charge there is left in the batteries.

When properly calibrated, battery monitors can account for all factors that affect battery state, including calculating the total charge delivered to the batteries, and subtracting the total charged used by the boat's systems. In addition to battery voltage, these monitors can display battery

▼ *A three- or four-stage battery charger will repay its initial cost several times over for boats that are regularly able to hook up to mains electricity.*

▲ Wind generators can produce plenty of power but some can be very noisy. Unless the charge from the generator is regulated, batteries can become overcharged and in high winds the generator can become overheated.

▼ The latest hydrogenerators are hugely efficient and easy to deploy.

charge/discharge current; state of charge of the battery in Amp-hours (Ah) or in percentage of total capacity; and time to go until the battery needs to be recharged.

Additional information available includes the average depth of discharge, depth of deepest discharge; number of charge/discharge cycles and number of occasions on which an under-voltage alarm has been triggered.

Alternative charging inputs

With many boats running numerous electrical devices, keeping the batteries topped up on a long passage, or during a period at anchor, can be a challenge. However, there are now many options that mean there should be no need to rely on the engine for this. In the past, wind generators were the mainstay for the power needs of many long-term cruisers and still have their fans today. However, they also have a number of drawbacks – when sailing downwind, for instance, the reduction in the apparent wind speed means their output is quite low.

The cost of solar panels has fallen rapidly and they are increasingly becoming the primary means of charging on many boats. On passage, this can be supplemented by further inputs from a towed generator, or from the type of hydro-generator that's increasingly common to see on long-distance racing yachts.

▼ Towed generators are less convenient, but cheaper, than hydrogenerators and can supply all power needed for long passages.

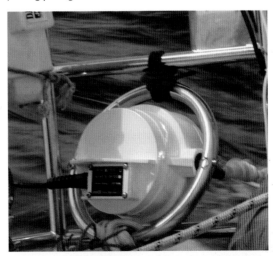

Common electrical problems

Most problems with marine electrical systems arise from four possible sources: a lack of maintenance, a poor standard of initial installation, insufficient battery capacity, or ineffective charging systems.

Water ingress is a frequent issue – salt water can corrode contacts very quickly. If connections are not scrupulously clean – or are loose – resistance will be increased, resulting in progressively reduced power. Contacts should be cleaned with wet and dry paper until the surface is shiny. Investigate any evidence of water ingress and eliminate the source. Also make sure you don't confuse a battery that's almost at the end of its life with one that is simply flat. The old battery may give reasonable voltage readings after charging, but these will fall rapidly when even a small load is drawn and the battery will soon be flat again.

▼ *Make sure you carry a full set of spare fuses. Even if your boat has circuit breakers on the switch panel, it's likely to have fuses protecting individual items of equipment.*

Fault finding

This is essentially a case of using logic to eliminate as many potential causes of failure as possible. Occasionally a large dose of perseverance is needed to identify an obscure problem, but equally it's really easy to overlook an obvious problem, so always start with the basics.

In the case of a non-functioning navigation light, for example, the first action should be to check the fuse or circuit breaker. If not the fuse or breaker, the problem is likely to be a defective bulb, so examine the old one. If it's blown – shown by a break in the thin filaments within the glass case – it can easily be replaced.

If the bulb appears to be intact, a voltmeter can be used to measure the voltage at the contacts in the lamp unit. If there's power at the switch panel, but not at the unit, you'll need to trace the wiring and attempt to locate the break in the circuit. How easy this is to find will depend on the individual boat – some boats may have a

▼ *Using a meter to check the power supply to a non-functioning interior light.*

number of joins in the wire. In any case, a boat with separate red and green pulpit lights will have a junction box somewhere near the bow, where the single supply from the distribution panel divides to take power to the two separate lamps. There will similarly be a junction somewhere for the feed to the stern light.

A meter can also be used on its resistance (Ω) setting to check whether or not a component is damaged. At the most basic level, electrical current must flow through the component in order for it to work. The resistance function of the meter passes a small current through the device being tested. If no current flows, it records infinite resistance (often shown as a figure 1 on the left-hand side of a digital meter display), telling us the component doesn't work. Note that components must be isolated from the boat's 12V supply before testing for resistance.

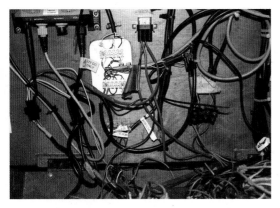

▲ The standards of marine electrical installations have often lagged behind those of the automotive industry, which means reliability suffers.

▼ A tablet computer in a waterproof and impact-resistant case is a useful backup.

Coping with power failure

Although in most cases this will not be a direct emergency situation, it's vital to establish clear priorities, especially if close to other traffic or navigation hazards. At night it's crucial to be seen by other vessels, so shining a bright torch or portable searchlight on the sails will help. Equally, don't forget to keep white handheld collision warning flares somewhere they can be found easily.

A handheld GPS, with waypoints downloaded to its memory, is a useful backup, as are paper charts covering the area in which you're sailing, plus any ports of refuge that may be needed if weather conditions turn severe. Similarly, chart-plotting software for smartphones and tablets is a great backup, but it's important to be conscious of the rapid drain on the battery when the device is used for this purpose. If it's not possible to restore power quickly, ration the use of electric devices to the minimum necessary for safe navigation and consistent with being visible to other traffic at night.

▲ Whatever you use as primary navigation tools, it's worth having a number of levels of backup and paper charts are vital.

Tools and spares

The number and complexity of tools that are carried on board will vary with the scope of voyages you undertake. However, even a boat that's only used for short day trips must carry sufficient tools and spares to fix basic engine, electrical and rigging problems. It's also worth carrying the manuals and parts diagrams for all the equipment you carry on board, from winches to refrigeration.

The greater the distances you travel with a boat, the greater the degree of self sufficiency that's required, which inevitably means getting involved in progressively more maintenance and repairs.

A comprehensive and well-organised tool kit and supply of spares therefore becomes increasingly essential, both for routine maintenance and to deal with unexpected breakages and failures. It's rarely sensible to attempt to economise when buying tools as more expensive items are invariably easier to use, which makes for a quicker and better result and will last a lifetime with proper care.

Tools should be stowed in a dry place that's also easily accessible, but the practicalities of most boats means it's inevitable that most tools and spares will be stowed in less than ideal locations. However, it's helpful to have a few frequently used items easily to hand, such as in a chart table drawer.

It's also important to consider the weight of tools, which can be considerable – ideally they should be stowed low down and close to the centre of the boat. They should be strapped down so that heavy toolboxes can't start flying around the cabin in a big sea or if the boat gets knocked down by wave action.

General tools:

- Allen keys
- Bolt cutters
- Bradawl
- Centre punch
- Chisels
- Drills – hand and powered plus drill bits for wood and metal, including stainless steel
- Files – wood and metal
- Hacksaws – large, small + spare tungsten carbide blades
- Hammers – 2lb lump + plastic mallet
- Hole cutters
- Knives – craft, palette + spare blades
- Mastic gun
- Mole wrench
- Multi-tool – eg Leatherman
- Oilstone for sharpening blades
- Pliers – various sizes and types, including circlip pliers
- Screwdrivers, various sizes and types
- Screwdriver bits, various sizes and types including Torx bits
- Socket sets – both half-inch and quarter-inch drives with metric and imperial sockets as appropriate
- Spanners, open ended, ring and adjustable types
- Tap and die set
- Torches, including a head torch
- Vernier gauge
- Vice – the type designed to fit on top of a winch is ideal
- Wire brush
- Wood saw

▲ Cordless power tools make it easier than ever before to carry out maintenance and repairs afloat.

General spares:
- Adhesives
- Abrasive paper (in various grades)
- Duct tape
- Hose clips in a range of sizes
- Marine grade sealant
- Masking tape
- Petroleum jelly (Vaseline)
- PTFE tape
- Spray can of lubricant
- Stainless steel nuts, bolts and screws in a range of sizes
- Washers (including large penny washers)

Rigging and sail repair tools:
- Cutting board
- Hot knife
- Rigging cutters
- Sailmaker's needles – it's worth noting that many of these are sized for ropework and only the smallest sizes tend to be suitable for sail repairs
- Sailmaker's palm
- Sharp knife – consider a ceramic one as these maintain an edge for longer
- Splicing fids
- Swedish fid

Rigging and sail making supplies:
- Blocks, including a snatch block
- Dyneema line – 2mm and 4mm
- Electrical tape
- Sailmaker's thread
- Self-adhesive sail repair patches
- Self-amalgamating tape
- Shackles in a range of sizes
- Spinnaker repair tape
- Whipping twine

Electrical tools:
- Crimping tool
- Electrical pliers
- Multimeter
- Precision (small) screwdriver set
- Soldering iron
- Wire cutters

Electrical spares:
- Cable ties
- Electrical tape
- Fuses
- Heat-shrink tubing
- Light bulbs, including navigation lights
- Solder
- Spare battery terminals
- Torch batteries
- Wire terminals and connectors
- Wire of different sizes

Engine tools:
- Feeler gauge
- Filter wrench
- Injector spanners
- Oil change pump
- Sparkplug spanner for outboard motor
- Torque wrench

▼ Boats that travel longer distances need to be self sufficient, with a wide range of tools and spares.

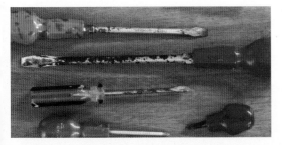

▲ One or two screwdrivers are unlikely to do every job – you need a wide range of different types and sizes.

Safety and emergency equipment

These are items that you will hope never to use, but will be really glad to have if you do encounter problems. As such they can often be likened to the seat belts or airbags in a car. Emergency equipment includes the liferaft, distress flares, EPIRBs, personal locator beacons and other man overboard equipment, lifejackets, harnesses and fire-fighting gear. However, unlike automotive safety features, these are not 'fit and forget' items – all require periodic maintenance and may have only a limited service life.

It's worth noting that, while items of a higher specification are likely to be needed for longer-distance voyaging, even in regions that have the benefit of comprehensive rescue cover a boat that only ever sails a few miles offshore needs to be capable of a high degree of self-sufficiency, especially at night, as search and rescue services won't be able to reach you immediately.

▼ Safety kit on a boat is never a 'fit and forget' item – it needs regular inspection and maintenance.

Lifejackets and buoyancy aids recommendations

Maritime rescue organisations throughout the world strongly recommend that appropriate lifejackets or buoyancy aids (collectively referred to as personal flotation devices or pfds) should be worn at all times when afloat. In some countries this is a legal requirement. Most sports governing bodies agree, but some recommend that pfds should always be worn, unless the user is sure they don't need to.

A pfd should be:
- regularly inspected for wear and tear.
- serviced in accordance with the manufacturer's recommendations.

Lifejacket or buoyancy aid?

The basic difference between the two types of pfd is that a buoyancy aid has in-built buoyancy and is intended for use as an aid to swimming, usually while engaged in a watersports activity in which it's expected that you will spend some time in the water. Buoyancy aids tend to be sold with 50 or 100N of flotation.

A lifejacket, however, is designed to turn an unconscious person face upwards when floating

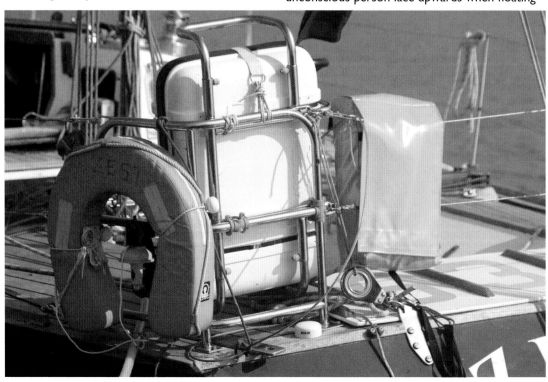

in the water. Most models used for recreational boating are inflatable types that only work once inflated, and will have buoyancy ratings of 150N or more (see p114–116 for more on flotation ratings). Wearing a properly fitted lifejacket can multiply survival times by a factor of 10–15, especially if it's fitted with a spray hood.

Buoyancy aids are recommended for water sports such as canoeing, dinghy sailing, kayaking, kitesurfing, paddling sports, personal watercraft (jet-skis), wake boarding, waterskiing and windsurfing. By contrast, lifejackets are used for applications in which you have no intention of falling into the water, such as motor cruisers, open boats including RIBs and small powerboats, sailing yachts and tenders.

▼ It's important to understand the differences between buoyancy aids and proper lifejackets.

TIPS

- Ensure everyone aboard your vessel has a suitable pfd.
- Ensure children wear pfds designed for their chest size and weight.
- Always use a good quality lifejacket that fits you properly.
- Choose a manual plus automatic inflation lifejacket with a light and spray hood.
- Always wear crotch straps with a lifejacket.
- Remember a buoyancy aid is only an aid to keeping you afloat.
- A level 150N or larger lifejacket is designed to turn an unconscious person face up.
- Keep your pfd regularly serviced.
- Carry spare automatic inflating mechanisms and CO_2 gas cylinders aboard.
- Check your country's laws about wearing personal flotation afloat.

▼ Despite recent advances in high-tech distress signalling systems, a set of distress flares remains a vital part of any boat's equipment.

Buoyancy

The level of buoyancy of a pfd is measured in Newtons (N).

A level 50 buoyancy aid is recommended for dinghy, kayak, windsurfing and personal watercraft users. It does not have sufficient buoyancy to protect a person who is unable to help themselves and will not turn a person who is lying face down in the water onto their back to allow them to breathe.

A level 100 pfd is recommended for use in sheltered and calm water. It is intended for those who may have to wait for rescue but are likely to do so in calm water conditions. It is not designed to have sufficient buoyancy to protect someone who is unable to help

themselves and will not roll an unconscious person on their back, particularly if they are wearing heavy clothing.

A level 150 lifejacket is recommended for general use on coastal and inshore waters when sailing, motorboating and fishing. It is intended for general offshore and rough weather use and should turn an unconscious person on to their back, with no subsequent action needed by the wearer to keep their face out of the water. Performance may be affected, however, if the user is wearing heavy and/or waterproof clothing.

A level 275 lifejacket is recommended for offshore cruising, fishing and commercial users. It is intended primarily for extreme conditions and for those wearing heavy protected clothing that

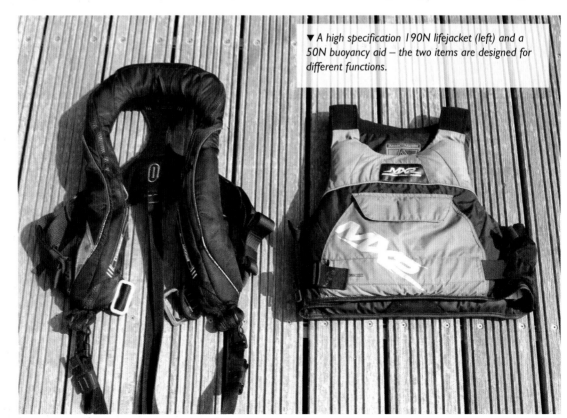

▼ A high specification 190N lifejacket (left) and a 50N buoyancy aid – the two items are designed for different functions.

may adversely affect the self-righting capacity of lower Newton-rated lifejackets. This lifejacket is designed to ensure that the wearer is floating in the correct position with their mouth and nose clear of the surface of the water.

Additional essential features

The following additional features are often incorporated in lifejackets of 150N specification and above; however this is not universally the case, especially with older models.

Crotch straps prevent the lifejacket riding up over your head when inflated, rendering it useless.

Spray hoods will keep your face clear of waves and spray that tend to wash over your head and are an essential feature.

Lights are essential for spotting a casualty in the water at night. Units designed for lifejackets are water-activated, which means they switch on automatically when necessary.

Even those who intend to sail only in daylight should have lights fitted to their lifejackets, as a problem encountered on a evening sail an hour or two before dusk can easily result in the boat returning to harbour after dark.

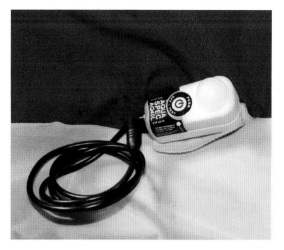

▲ The lifejacket light is an important safety feature and should be checked at every service.

▼ The spray hood is designed to keep water off your face to allow you to breathe if you fall in.

▼ Lifejackets that weren't originally supplied with crotch straps can be retrofitted with them if necessary.

Lifejacket care

It's all too easy to be complacent about the condition of lifejackets, but up to one-third of the lifejackets Britain's Royal National Lifeboat Institution inspects as part of its Sea Check service are found to have at least one significant fault. Fortunately, it's easy to check your own lifejackets and attend to the most common problems. In addition to the annual service specified by most manufacturers, the RNLI recommends more frequent inspections, with some items checked at least monthly.

1. Inflate the jacket using the oral inflation tube every six months – the jacket should retain air pressure for 24 hours.
2. If the jacket passes the inflation test, give it a thorough visual examination. In particular, look for signs of chafe or abrasion from the gas bottle, as well as any other types of damage to the casing or surface of the air chamber. Pay particular attention to the seams and the points at which the oral inflation tube and inflation activation devices are joined to the jacket.
3. Every three months, check for wear and tear of straps, belts, harnesses and other webbing items, paying particular attention to the stitching. At the same time, check the condition and operation of all buckles, zips, Velcro or other securing for the outer cover, and any other fastenings. The condition of the retro-reflective tape is also important – is it free from cracks and other degradation and well adhered to the jacket?

▼ *Pump the lifejacket up to see if it retains air for 24 hours and check the condition of the reflective tape.*

▲ *Old and new lifejacket inflation cylinders.*

Gas cylinders

The cylinders that contain the CO_2 gas used to inflate the lifejacket can easily work loose and should be checked for tightness at least every month, although a quick check each day the jacket is used is even better. The importance of this simple task cannot be overstressed – it's the most common reason for lifejacket failure. Every three months, cylinders should be examined for signs of corrosion, and replaced if any is in evidence. Double-check the lifejacket material in all areas that have been in contact with a rusting cylinder – damage to the material is common.

Every 12 months, remove the cylinder to check for any other signs of damage and replace if necessary. With the cylinder removed, check that the manually operated activation lever functions smoothly and easily.

Weigh the cylinder on digital scales. The gross weight (ie the combined weight of the cylinder itself, plus the compressed gas it contains) should be stamped on the side of the cylinder. If the actual weight does not match this figure, the cylinder should be replaced.

When renewing cylinders, make sure you use one of the correct size – they are available in a range of sizes from 16–60g. Standard adult 150N jackets take a 33g bottle, while children's models generally take a 24g unit. A 275N lifejacket will need a 60g gas bottle.

When replacing the cylinder, carefully screw it into the activating unit by hand and ensure it is tight. It's important to follow the instructions in your lifejacket's manual at this stage to ensure all elements are properly assembled – there are important differences between models. Note also that the cylinder should be placed inside its protective sleeve, to reduce chafing and abrasion of the air chamber.

Conventional automatic inflation devices gather moisture over time, so it's possible for a lifejacket to inflate prematurely if it has been continually exposed to damp conditions. For this reason they should be replaced annually. They also have a finite shelf life and should not be used once the expiry date on the device is reached.

Hydrostatic (Hammar) type auto-inflate lifejackets require a different procedure, as the gas cylinder is within the air chamber. It's therefore protected from the elements and should not rust. The activation devices also have a longer service life, needing to be replaced only every three to five years.

▼ Check whether the inflation bottle is fully screwed in as often as possible – this is the biggest single cause of lifejacket failure.

TIP

Service life and storage
The average lifespan of a lifejacket is 10 years, although cheaper models intended for occasional use may have a life expectancy of only half that figure. If stored for any length of time, for instance at the end of the season, lifejackets should be rinsed with fresh water and dried, then partially inflated and hung on a non-metallic coat hanger. This will prevent damage of the air chamber along the line of folds and creases.

▲ Stitching of lifejackets and harnesses should be of a contrasting colour to make it easy to check for damage.

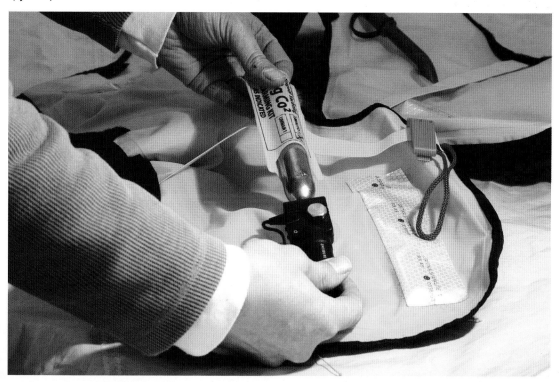

Safety harnesses and jackstays

The old cliché that prevention is better than cure is particularly apt for man overboard situations and it's crucial to give due thought to making certain everyone stays on board. It is the skipper's responsibility to decide when safety harnesses should be worn. The type of vessel, sea state, weather conditions and crew experience should be considered. For example, if a crew member (young or old) has poor balance or lacks experience at sea, they should be clipped on sooner.

Motor vessels should also be equipped with at least a couple of harnesses and suitable points for clipping on. While their crews are less likely to need to go on deck in rough weather, it is by no means an impossibility. A common example is the need to go to the foredeck to secure a tow line following engine failure.

▲ It's important to have a strong point near the companionway for attaching harness lines.

Generally, wear safety harnesses:

- In a rough sea state when on deck or in the cockpit
- When sails are reefed due to wind strength
- When alone on deck
- At night in all conditions
- When using a spinnaker
- In fog

It's also important for skippers to encourage their crew members to build up a constant awareness of potential dangers, as well as looking out for other people, especially those who are less experienced or able.

The aim of the harness is to keep crew members on board should they slip or fall while on deck or in the cockpit. If someone does fall overboard when attached to the boat with a harness line they will be towed through the water face downwards and will immediately find it difficult to breathe. In this event it's vital to take way off the boat as quickly as possible, by turning up into the wind or heaving to. If using a spinnaker, the quickest way to douse it is to cut the guy (or tack line for an asymmetric sail), halyard and sheet, in that order, with a sharp knife.

Jackstays and strong points

The aim is to clip on to a part of the boat from which your harness line is too short for you to slip over the side and into the water. This generally means strong points near the companionway and in the cockpit, together with jackstays along each side deck. Clipping to the windward jackstay will mean that, if you fall, your harness line should come up tight before you slip out under the rail on the lee side of the boat. Companionway strong points should be positioned such that it's possible to clip on before emerging from the safety of the cabin and unclip only once securely below, with your feet on the cabin floor.

▼ Jackstays must be firmly attached to the boat – they may be subjected to loads of close to one tonne.

Both jackstays and strong points can be subjected to considerable loads if someone falls in the water and the system needs to be able to withstand a safe working load of around one tonne. The webbing therefore needs to be in good condition and strong points securely attached to the boat, with big backing pads or penny washers under the deck to spread the load through the structure. It's worth noting that regulations for longer-distance offshore races require enough strong points to be fitted that no more than one-third of the crew needs to be clipped to the jackstay.

Harness lines should be periodically checked for chafe, damage to stitching and correct operation of the clips. More recent harness lines also have a 'flag' incorporated that indicates when they have been subjected to a high load and should be replaced. Similarly, webbing jackstays should be checked for chafe periodically and if they are more than ten years old they should be replaced due to likely UV degradation.

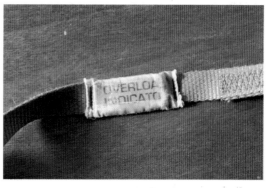

▲ A harness line with a 'flag' that indicates when it has been subject to load and therefore needs to be replaced.

▼ Familiarity with using a harness makes it easy to work efficiently while staying safe.

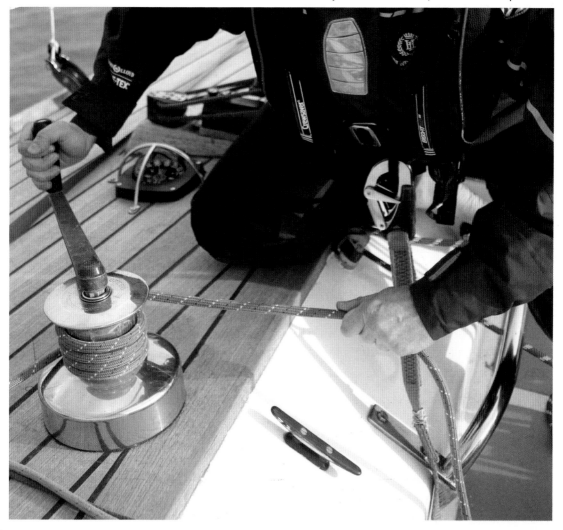

Lifebuoys, dan buoys and lights

Time is critical in the event of a man overboard emergency, so it's important to have all the items needed immediately to hand. Lifebuoys should be mounted on quick release brackets within easy reach of the helm position. It's also worth having a man overboard button for a GPS unit or chartplotter within reach of the helm, as getting an accurate position at the exact time of the incident can help speed up a search enormously if you lose sight of the casualty.

Lifebuoys should be fitted with a drogue to prevent them being blown downwind of the casualty, as well as strobe lights and marine grade retro-reflective tape for use at night. They should also have the boat's name on them in case they are lost overboard and found by another vessel. If a lifebuoy does not have a boat's name on it, a search could be started unnecessarily. It goes without saying that all crew should know the location of the lifebuoys on board and know how to release them quickly in case of a man overboard emergency.

Having two lifebuoys means that, if the casualty fails to reach the first, you can pass by a little upwind and throw the second almost into his arms. If the casualty is not wearing a lifejacket, this can buy a little precious time to prepare the boat for the actual rescue – for instance, furling the headsail and checking there are no lines in the water before starting the engine.

Dan buoys

A dan buoy is a 2m high floating pole with a flag and light on top that is attached to a lifebuoy to make it visible from a greater distance. A dan buoy should be mounted alongside the lifebuoy in the cockpit, ready for instant deployment. Inflatable models that are easy to stow and will inflate within a few seconds of hitting the water are popular for obvious reasons, but must be regularly inspected and serviced in a similar manner to lifejackets.

Lifebuoy lights and searchlights

Conventional lifebuoy lights are prone to being unreliable, so should be checked at the beginning of each passage, and spare bulbs and batteries

▼ An inflatable dan buoy is easy to stow but must be serviced in a similar manner to lifejackets.

▼ A searchlight has multiple uses.

▲ *A waterproof torch that floats with the lens pointing upwards is a good supplement to lifebuoy lights.*

need to be carried on board. Sealed-for-life types, which typically have a non-replaceable battery with a five-year life, are generally much more reliable and are therefore worth the modest additional investment.

It's also a good idea to keep a powerful floating torch on deck that can be thrown in the water to mark the casualty's position in the event of the lifebuoy light not working. In any case, even in benign conditions, a man overboard at night is possibly the biggest challenge any skipper might face and the more pointers you have the better the chances of a successful outcome.

Searchlights can also help considerably with locating a casualty in the dark. Modern battery technology means these no longer need to be tethered by a power cable – the best cordless models are capable of producing a bright light for a considerable length of time. This means it's easier for a crew member to hold the unit out over the side of the boat, thus minimising the glare and reflection that can easily destroy night vision.

Throwing lines and rescue slings

A 20m-long floating line, commonly sold in a weighted bag that makes it easy to accurately throw over long distances, means you won't need to stop the boat directly next to a casualty in the water. It's much easier to stop the boat nearby, then throw a line to them. The line should be flaked into the bag so it runs out smoothly, not coiled; however, many are sold with the line coiled – it's worth checking!

A rescue sling (sometimes referred to as a lifesling) is a foam horseshoe on the end of a 20m-long floating line that can also be thrown to a casualty in the water. In some cases it's also possible to tow it behind the boat, circling the casualty in the same way that a waterski boat driver does to return the tow line to a water skier after they have fallen in the water.

▲ *Rescue slings can make it much easier to make contact with a man overboard and can facilitate getting them back on board.*

▲ *Make sure the rope is properly flaked into the bag for the throwing line – if it's coiled, it will tangle.*

Distress signals

Modern communications have revolutionised distress signalling – a few hundred pounds will buy a GPS enabled EPIRB that will beam a distress message, including the boat's exact position, from anywhere in the world to a maritime rescue coordination centre, via a satellite. If the EPIRB has been properly registered (a legal requirement) then information about the boat and an on-shore contact is also available to the rescue coordinators.

For craft sailing closer to shore, a VHF radio with a DSC facility enables a distress message, including the craft's position, to be sent a distance of up to around 30 miles at the touch of a button.

▲ For most boats, a VHF radio with a DSC function and GPS input is the first choice for raising the alarm in a distress situation...

▼ ...however, distress flares remain important, especially for pinpointing the exact location of your boat.

Mayday definitions

A Mayday situation is defined as one in which a vessel, or person(s), is in grave and imminent danger. It's important to signal distress as soon as possible once an emergency has occurred. A good example of this is man overboard – there can be no doubt that a crew member floating offshore in cold water is in 'grave and imminent' danger, so a Mayday call should be made immediately. Coastguards would much rather stand down a rescue operation than, as occasionally happens, be called when it is too late for them to be of help.

If in a situation where the boat or a person is in danger, but that danger is neither grave nor imminent, it may still be worthwhile informing the Coastguard. The correct form for this is a Pan Pan call – the call is identical to a Mayday, but with the word Mayday replaced by Pan Pan.

Distress flares

Older technology is also useful and distress flares remain essential for pinpointing a vessel's exact position during a search and rescue operation. Flares should be kept in a waterproof container in an easily accessible location.

There are several types of flare for different purposes and it's worth noting that different brands have very different firing mechanisms. Given that the right time to read the instructions for the first time is not in the middle of an

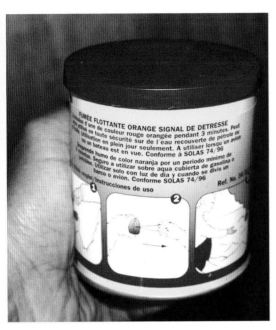

▲ *Make sure you check out and remember the firing procedure for the flares on each boat you sail.*

emergency situation on a dark, windy and wet night, the only way to be sure of how to operate the flares is by examining them on each boat you sail on. Expiry dates can also be checked at the same time – generally, flares have a shelf life of around three years.

Red handheld flares are used as a line of sight distress signal by day and night, with maximum visibility of around 3–5 miles (5–8km). Hold with an outstretched arm, pointing the flare downwind, and avoid looking at the flare.

Orange smoke flares are used as a line of sight distress signal for daytime use only, although they may also be seen by aircraft passing overhead, providing the cloud base is sufficiently high. They are available in handheld versions that last for around 60 seconds, or in the form of a larger floating canister that burns for approximately three minutes.

Red parachute or rocket flares, used for longer range distress signalling, are visible for around 10 miles (16km) in daylight and up to 40 miles (64km) at night. If fired vertically they can reach a height of 300m (984ft), but fire them at 45 degrees downwind in low cloud or strong winds. Burn time is less than one minute.

TIPS

- Handheld flares get very hot. Keep a pair of leather gloves with the container to prevent burns.
- Check expiry dates and take advice on disposal of out of date flares locally.
- All crew should know the location of the flares on board and know how to operate them.

White handheld flares are available in some countries and are used to signal your position at night if there is a risk of collision. As with red handheld flares, hold with arms outstretched, pointing the flare downwind and don't look at the light. Lasts for around one minute.

Given the relatively short length of time for which most flares burn, it's usual to deploy them in pairs, firing the second one around a minute after the first. This allows an observer to confirm the sighting and use a hand-bearing compass to get a position line on the casualty. The exception to this is with orange smoke flares, as the cloud of smoke tends to linger for some time after the flare itself has burned out.

▲ *Flares have a shelf life of around three years, after which they must be replaced.*

▼ *EPIRBs and PLBs are an excellent choice for raising the alarm when you are beyond VHF range.*

Liferafts

A liferaft is an essential piece of equipment to carry on offshore or coastal passages and should be regularly serviced by professionals according to manufacturers' recommendations. They should be stowed where they are ready for immediate launching. All crew should know the location of the liferaft and know how to launch, inflate and board it. They should also know what equipment it contains.

Types of liferaft

There are two international standards for liferafts – SOLAS and ISO 9650. SOLAS are heavier duty types and may not always be suitable for pleasure craft. There are two categories of ISO 9650 – 'Type 1' for offshore navigation and 'Type 2' for coastal navigation.

Skippers should ensure that their vessel is fitted with a liferaft that is designed to cope with the conditions they will encounter, is equipped accordingly and can accommodate all crew. Equipment will vary depending on whether the raft is specified for survival periods of less than, or more than, 24 hours. However, in all cases the equipment packed in the raft will be of only a very basic level. This is why it's important to also have a grab bag of essentials available, as well as emergency water in a portable container.

Typical liferaft contents

Basic specification:
- 2 paddles
- 2 red hand flares
- Bailer and sponge
- Waterproof torch
- Whistle
- Lifesaving signal cards
- Floating knife
- Drogue (sea anchor)
- Repair kit
- 6 x seasickness tablets per person
- Rescue quoit with 30m floating line
- Top-up pump

ISAF specification:
- As above, plus:
- Water pack
- Additional flares
- First aid kit
- Thermal protective aids
- Signalling mirror
- Seasickness bags

▼ Liferafts packed inside a fibreglass canister can be kept outside, which makes it easy to launch them quickly.

Grab bag

In the event of having to abandon ship, it is recommended to have a designated waterproof dry bag to carry essential emergency items. These might include items already in use on the boat, as well as some already stored in the bag. Minimum grab bag contents include a handheld GPS, handheld VHF, PLB or EPIRB, flares, seasickness pills, duplicate medication for any crew members that rely on regular medicinal drugs, torch and batteries, first aid kit, thermal protective aids, water, ship's documents and personal documents such as passports.

It's worth noting that the biggest dangers to survivors in a liferaft are from exposure and dehydration. Even in the height of summer, in north European and North American waters it's possible to die from hypothermia within a few hours, so staying dry and having a suitable supply of warm clothes are the most important priorities.

Next is the need for water – while it's possible for a healthy adult to survive for a few days without water, deterioration is rapid. However, we can survive with no food for much longer – up to a month in some cases – so food is much lower on the priority list than is generally realised. By the same token, a means of signalling distress – ideally an EPIRB – should be very much higher on the list.

▼ *Liferafts packed in a soft valise must be stowed below deck or in a dry locker. However, you should be able to launch the unit over the rail within 15 seconds.*

This is a summary of the minimum grab bag contents the International Sailing Federation (ISAF) recommends for vessels used offshore:

Grab bag contents

- Flares: 2 red parachute, 2 red hand flares and cyalume-type chemical light sticks
- Watertight handheld Electronic Position Fixing System (eg GPS)
- SART (Search and Rescue Transponder)
- Combined 406MHz/121.5MHz or type 'E' EPIRB
- Water in resealable containers or a hand-operated desalinator plus containers for water
- Watertight handheld marine VHF transceiver plus a spare set of batteries
- Watertight flashlight with spare batteries and bulb
- Dry suits or thermal protective aids or survival bags
- Second sea anchor for liferaft with swivel and >30m line diameter >9.5mm
- 2 safety tin openers (if appropriate)
- First-aid kit including at least 2 tubes of sunscreen. Dressings should be capable of being effectively used in wet conditions. The kit should be clearly marked and resealable
- Signalling mirror
- High-energy food
- Nylon string, polythene bags, seasickness tablets (minimum 6 per person)
- Watertight handheld aviation VHF transceiver (if race area warrants)
- Medical supplies including any for pre-existing medical conditions of any crew member
- Spare unbreakable spectacles for any crew members needing them

▼ *Essential items for a grab bag include a torch, handheld VHF, GPS, EPIRB or PLB, passports and boat documents.*

Electronics and instruments

▲ *A radar reflector is one of the few items boats are required to carry by international law.*

Modern systems are capable of providing a huge amount of information that can make passages quicker and safer. However, one of the first principles is to be sure that other vessels can see you, especially at night or in poor visibility.

Radar reflector

This is one of the most important safety devices you can have on a boat – and it's one of the very few requirements in international maritime law. Radar reflectors help to increase the visibility of a vessel to craft fitted with radar sets. The UK's Maritime & Coastguard Agency (MCA), for instance, advises they are fitted to all small craft to help avoid collisions, as this extract from Marine Guidance Note MGN 349 clearly states:

'It is strongly recommended that: the requirements of SOLAS Chapter V Regulation 19 are complied with [and] yachtsmen permanently install, not just carry on-board, a radar reflector or RTE that offers the largest Radar Cross Section (RCS) practicable for their vessel. In addition, small craft owners and operators are strongly recommended to fit the best performing radar reflector possible. It is also essential for skippers to be aware that, notwithstanding the type of radar reflector fitted, in certain circumstances their craft may still not be readily visible on ships' radars. They should navigate with caution'.

As with VHF antennas, reflectors benefit from being fitted aloft as radar works on a line of sight basis, so the higher the reflector the greater the distance it can be seen.

Active radar reflectors

Even the best passive radar reflectors may fail to return a reliable and strong signal, especially in large waves, in periods of rain or at long distance. An active radar reflector is an electronic device that amplifies the return signal, making it many times stronger and thereby ensuring your boat is seen as a solid target on other vessels' radar displays.

These tend to be relatively low-power devices, typically consuming less than half an amp of current. Two types are generally available to return signals from either or from both S and X band radars – the two types fitted to large commercial vessels. However, as yet there is not a product that also returns a signal from the (confusingly named) 3G and 4G 'Broadband' units that are becoming increasingly popular for recreational craft.

▼ *An electronic active radar reflector returns a much stronger and more reliable signal.*

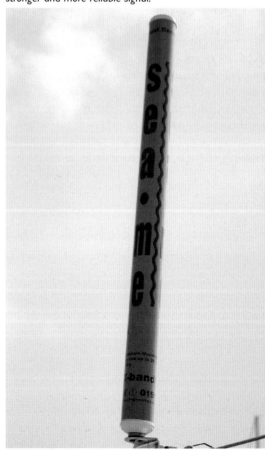

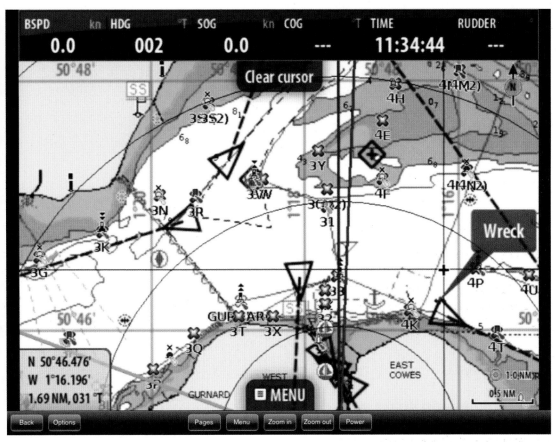

AIS and radar

For some time, ships of over 300 tonnes, all passenger vessels and many fishing boats have been required to carry an Automatic Identification System that broadcasts details including their name, position, course and speed at frequent intervals.

Other vessels equipped with an AIS receiver can get this information, while the unit will also calculate your closest point of approach (CPA) to other vessels, the time until the CPA is reached, and the bearing of the vessel. This can be a great help to skippers of leisure boats, especially at night, in reduced visibility, or when crossing busy shipping lanes.

However, it's important to recognise that while an AIS receiver does not do everything that a radar set does (it's a collision warning device, not a navigational system), it actually does some things better, such as providing detailed information on shipping and requires a less skilled operator to elicit the information available. In addition to

▲ AIS can be an exceptionally useful aid to identifying the risk of collision with large vessels, providing a degree of advance warning both at night and in reduced visibility.

the vessels equipped with the mandatory (Class A) AIS systems, an increasing number of smaller craft, including yachts, are fitting the optional AIS Class B systems, which means they are visible to any craft carrying an AIS receiver.

As with other electronics, radar sets for the leisure marine sector are becoming more compact, affordable and sophisticated. In particular, many now offer ARPA (Automatic Radar Plotting Aid) functions that can be used to monitor a number of vessels that might be of concern.

On the downside, using a radar still requires a skilled operator to avoid tuning out smaller targets lost in wave clutter or in rain showers. Interpreting the radar picture is also a skilled role to avoid the danger of a radar-assisted collision.

Instruments and chart plotters

GPS enabled chart plotters may have done more to change the experience of boating than any other device – being able to constantly see exactly where the boat is, and where it's heading, at any moment in time is revolutionary.

However, evolution continues in this respect and in the parlance of today's marine electronics industry, the humble chart plotter has been replaced by the Multi-Function Display. This is a unit that can display any information sent to it, including charts, with AIS and/or radar overlays, and data from the instrument system and engine monitoring. MFDs increasingly form the hub of any instrument system and can display and control an ever-wider range of inputs. There are also ongoing moves to simplify user interfaces, often borrowing from the gestures used to operate smartphones and tablets.

Nevertheless, there are a few ways in which chart plotters have the potential to lead us into trouble. One is whether the datum used by the GPS unit matches that used by the charts, although WGS84 is the standardised norm and mismatches are less common than in the early days of GPS. A

▲ The ability to see exactly where we are at any time is revolutionary, but it's important to recognise that chart plotters are not infallible.

second is whether the charts are up to date – while it's easy (though time consuming) to add corrections to paper charts from Notices to Mariners, updating electronic charts is not so straightforward. Yet a chart folio that's even just a couple of years out of date may have dangerous inaccuracies.

Finally, in more remote parts of the world charts still rely on surveys carried out by sextant and compass in the 18th and 19th centuries. Here, the apparent accuracy of the chart plotter can be deceiving and you may know your position to a much greater degree of accuracy to that at which the chart is drawn.

Instrument systems

Modern systems can monitor a wide range of inputs and calculate further useful information such as the true wind speed and direction, again with the potential to show any data on any display. The depth sounder remains one of the most useful of all and has saved many a boat from running aground, even though it only provides historic information. However, forward-looking sounders that use a graphical display to show both the depth under the boat, and the depth ahead look set to become much more widely available over the next few years.

Boat speed and distance logs also give valuable information. Before GPS became ubiquitous, distance logs provided a key piece of navigational data and were one of the key elements for plotting the vessel's position. One of the big advances in the past few years is in the quality of displays, with the latest offering large and clear numbers that are easily read in bright sunlight and when wearing polarising sunglasses.

In addition, it is often useful to have instrument or chart plotter displays at the chart table below deck. In the past this meant investing in additional hardware; however, the main manufacturers now offer wifi networking that enables a tablet or smartphone to interface with the system and display any of the available data.

▲ Modern MFDs and instrument systems allow tablets and smartphones to interface over wifi networks.

▼ Smartphone and tablet navigation apps, backed up with paper charts, make for quick and easy position checks. Smartphones can also display wifi enabled instrument systems data.

▼ A depth sounder with a graphic display can give more information at a glance than just the raw number.

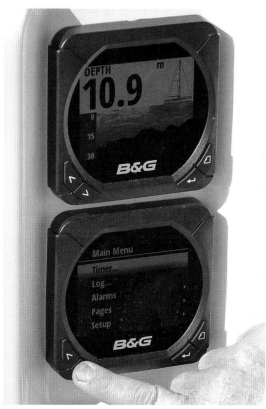

Calibration of instruments

Many boat owners are guilty of failing to give sufficient attention to calibration. This results in instrument systems that display inaccurate (and sometimes misleading) information – it's a classic 'garbage in-garbage out' scenario. In addition, more sophisticated autopilots are only as good as their inputs, so accurate calibration of the instrument system, including compass, masthead wind angle, and boat speed, is necessary.

The fundamentals of calibration are easy to grasp and implement, so there's no excuse for sailing with inaccurate data. It is, however, an iterative process, so getting really good results is an on-going process. It's worth rechecking calibration during the season in any case – weed growth can slow the paddlewheel used to measure boat speed, while moving ferrous items around the boat or installing additional electronics may affect the calibration of an electronic compass.

▲ Apparent wind angle is one of the key calibration settings.

▼ Think carefully about positioning pilot controls – the unit isn't as useful if you have to stand next to the wheel to make course changes.

There are only five key inputs of raw data: boat speed, compass heading, measured wind angle, measured wind speed and depth. These basic inputs are used to calculate all other data, including true and apparent wind speed and direction. Measured wind speed is generally a factory setting that's derived from wind tunnel testing, so doesn't need adjustment, while the calibration procedures for other data will be detailed in the manual for your instrument system.

Autopilots and self-steering

A decent self-steering system is a great safety feature if it will cope with steering in bad weather when crew members may become tired to the point of exhaustion, or seasick. However, a low-specification system that's used primarily to take over briefly while you're doing other tasks such as making a cup of tea, or to take the boredom out of motoring in a calm, is unlikely to do the job in challenging conditions.

A basic unit's lack of a rate sensing or gyro compass means that it is not able to respond quickly and will struggle to keep a boat on course, especially in a quartering sea. Also, the on-deck tiller pilots are vulnerable to failure as a result of water ingress. Therefore a below-deck unit, with a gyro or rate-sensing compass and separate pilot computer, is the ideal minimum specification.

There are also a couple of reasons why it's not worth skimping on a model that's only just large enough for your boat's published displacement.

▼ Wind instruments can be interfaced with a pilot to steer to either the apparent or true wind.

▲ *An autopilot can free you up to trim sails, attend to navigation or make a cup of tea.*

Firstly, larger models tend to turn the rudder faster, and thereby maintain a straighter course, as well as consuming less power. Secondly, most cruising boats, once loaded with supplies and crew, are relatively heavy compared to their published displacement – up to an extra 20 per cent is not unusual.

It's worth noting that even the best self-steering systems struggle with an unbalanced sail plan – so it's important to make sure sails are well trimmed and are reefed as necessary to suit the wind conditions.

All pilots have changeable settings that enable the system to steer the boat across a wide range of conditions – if you learn the settings for different conditions that work for your boat, you will get much better performance from the system.

▲ *On-deck tiller and wheel pilots are not as effective as their below-deck counterparts with separate pilot computers and rams.*

▼ *A gyro or rate-sensing compass will improve the performance of a pilot enormously.*

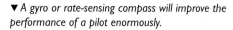

System networks

Just as it's important to have knowledge of your boat's engine, an understanding of the electronics systems will help you to troubleshoot any problems you encounter.

In the early days of marine electronics, each instrument had a specific function – there was the depth sounder, the boat speed log, the wind instrument and so on. While a few boats remain set up in this manner, the norm for the past couple of decades has been a networked system in which any of the system data can be displayed on any unit.

There are two industry standard data protocols used to allow products from different manufacturers to be interfaced with each other, so you aren't locked into buying from your existing instrument supplier. These are NMEA0183 and a later version, NMEA2000 (the latter often abbreviated to N2K). In electronics terms, both are old and therefore somewhat slow standards, although in most cases the volumes of data sent are small, so in practice this is rarely a problem for NMEA2000 systems. In addition, many manufacturers also have their own protocols, which may allow for data transfer up

to 20 times faster than NMEA protocols. Although NMEA0183 is now several decades old, there's still equipment on sale using this standard. It requires each instrument to be wired separately with five fine wires, which are prone to failure at the connections. N2K, by contrast, is a 'single wire' plug-and-play system in which equipment is connected to a backbone cable (or bus) that, if necessary, runs the length of the vessel.

For data transfer to take place, the backbone needs to have a resistor at each end. On many systems this is neatly incorporated in the masthead wind sensor for one end of the system. However, if there's a problem at the masthead – the sensors can be unreliable – the entire instrument system can be rendered inoperable.

An easy solution is to carry a spare terminal resistor, so that if the system goes down you can unplug the wind instrument and insert the resistor. If the system then works you have both identified the problem and still have most of the system's functionality.

▼ Plug-and-play connectors for an NMEA2000 network. It makes sense to label each wire so that you can trace its function for fault finding.

▲ *A spare handheld GPS is a convenient backup in the event of power failure, but make sure you have enough batteries.*

▼ *A handheld VHF can be useful to use on deck and as a backup, but make sure you charge it regularly.*

Backup equipment

Despite the proliferation of modern marine electronics, there remains a valid argument that the only items needed for a competent skipper to safely take a well-found boat anywhere in the world are a set of up-to-date paper charts, a lead line, distance log, sextant and compass.

However, all but a handful of ardent traditionalists choose to add additional equipment and more complex systems as it makes boating more fun, more convenient and safer. For instance, a chart plotter that shows exactly where you are when entering an unfamiliar harbour in the dark makes it much less likely that you will feel the need to heave to offshore until dawn.

Nevertheless, a problem comes when we rely on complex systems to such an extent that we would be, quite literally, lost without them. It's therefore important to still carry the basics on board so that you can revert to traditional navigation if necessary and to practice doing so.

On the other hand, while there's still no substitute for paper charts as an ultimate backup, today's technology also makes it possible to have more convenient intermediate backup equipment. For instance, an iPad or smartphone with suitable specification and with a suitable waterproof and impact-resistant case can be used as a chart plotter if loaded with a marine navigation app and appropriate charts.

▼ *Each end of the NMEA2000 backbone needs a terminal resistor. It's worth carrying a spare, particularly if your system has one built into the masthead wind sensor.*

Fresh-water system

On shore, we tend to take a reliable supply of clean fresh water for granted. However, the situation on a boat could not be more different, with the supply restricted for reasons including limited tankage. It's also important to consider and guard against the potential for contamination. For day trips with a small crew you won't need a lot of water, but even then it's important to have sufficient on board, especially in warm weather.

However, on longer trips the luxury of plentiful water tends to come with a hefty price tag, whether it's the upfront cost of a watermaker, plus its maintenance and power requirements, or simply a lack of space in which to install a large amount of tankage. The careful use of water therefore tends to be an important ongoing priority if you're on board for any length of time.

Even larger yachts fitted with watermakers normally depend on a supply of diesel to produce the electricity, either via the main engine or a separate generator, to power the device. However, the latest hydrogenerators and improvements in solar technology are starting to make it possible to power watermakers without running an engine or generator.

Boats venturing on longer voyages, or simply to more remote anchorages in which it's not so easy to pick up fresh water, need to be sure they carry sufficient supplies. When calculating the amount of water you need to carry for a particular passage, it's important to allow a contingency for delays or problems with the boat: carrying sufficient to cover emergency rations for a period of 50 per cent longer than the expected passage time is a sensible allowance.

In addition, it's prudent to carry an adequate spare supply of water in cans in case tanks become ruptured or contaminated. This can also double as the water earmarked for taking to the liferaft in the event of being forced to abandon ship.

It's worth measuring the size of the water tanks on your boat, as a surprising number differ significantly from the boatbuilders' standard figures. An accurate, though time-consuming method of doing this is to fill the tanks via cans of which you know the capacity. It's also important to remember that tank gauges, where fitted, tend to be very poorly calibrated, often indicating the tank is still full when it's almost half empty.

▼ Water systems can be surprisingly complex – this is a basic 30ft cruiser – so it's important to identify what each element of the system does.

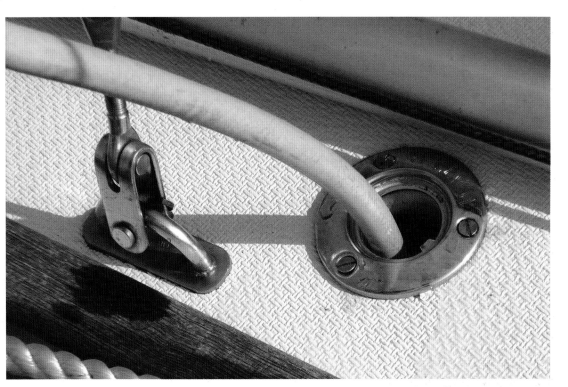

Keeping it fresh

There are also potential problems associated with storing fresh water in tanks for long periods, especially in warm weather. Good practice starts before you begin to fill the water tanks. For a start, beware of ends of hoses that have been allowed to fall into potentially dirty harbour water – these should be cleaned thoroughly before filling your tanks.

Unfortunately, unless it's used very frequently, carrying your own hose is not an automatic solution – on many boats the hose may not be used for weeks, or even months at a time, allowing any water that remains in it to stagnate and for mould and other microbes to form.

▲ When filling fresh water tanks avoid poking the hose into the filler, as has been done here, to prevent the water turning foul.

It's also worth tasting water before filling up – if it tastes bad then let the hose run for a little and try again. When you fill up, it's also better not to poke the end of the hose deep into the filler – instead hold it just above the filler.

A variety of treatment options are available to add to water tanks to eliminate the danger of bugs growing in the tank. It's also possible to fit microfilters that will not allow large bacteria to pass, although smaller microbes present in the water, including viruses, will also get through.

▼ Boats with two water tanks will have a changeover valve to switch between each one.

System maintenance and troubleshooting

Water pumps tend to be robust devices that are capable of operating for many years without trouble, particularly if there's a filter in the system ahead of the pump. However, they are not immune from wiring and other electrical supply problems and ultimately have a finite lifespan. Leaks from a tank or another part of the system, however, are more commonly encountered.

These can manifest in a number of ways, the most obvious being a flexible tank that wears a hole due to chafe, although even stainless steel tanks have the potential to develop pinholes that can be difficult to track down. If you encounter unexpected water in the bilge it's worth checking whether it's fresh or salty – the former indicates a likely leak from the fresh-water system. Since any kind of leak has the potential to drain water tanks, when on passage it's good practice to leave pressure pumps turned off whenever the system is not being used.

Winterising is an important element of maintenance that's all too frequently overlooked. Emptying the tanks before laying the boat up will prevent fresh water in them, and in electric pumps, from freezing.

Conserving water

Electric water pumps tend to be very wasteful of water and even the most cautious crew members can easily treble their consumption compared to using manual foot pumps. Fitting a manual pump also has the benefit of adding a layer of redundancy of systems that will improve reliability – if the boat suffers electrical power failure, or if the electric water pump fails, you will still be able to get water out of tanks. Equally a salt-water tap in the galley, again with a manual pump, will save on fresh water if you plan to venture well offshore.

Showers can be one of the biggest causes of water consumption on board; however, there are a few simple measures that can help to significantly reduce consumption, without unduly compromising comfort. The first is to fit a shower head that requires the user to hold a button down for water to flow – this means the water automatically stops when you pause to apply shampoo and so on. A more dramatic option is to replace the ubiquitous electric sump pump used to drain the shower compartment with a manually operated foot pump – this will immediately highlight to anyone using the shower the amount of water used.

▼ Manual foot pumps are easy to use, yet reduce consumption considerably and add a layer of redundancy.

Watermakers

Watermakers can appear to be an indispensable tool on long-term cruising boats, creating apparently limitless supplies of fresh water. Unlike most items of on-board equipment, they need least attention when used regularly, at least once every five days and preferably more frequently. However, if operated less frequently the system must be decommissioned to avoid the need to replace expensive membranes. In addition, they consume a large amount of electrical power – one reason that many boats with a watermaker also have a generator, although while on passage a towed generator would produce sufficient power.

The maintenance requirement of watermakers is not a reason in itself to avoid fitting one – with careful planning it needn't be an unduly onerous task; however, it's important to recognise the drawbacks as well as the benefits. This may sway the decision as to whether or not to fit one, especially for boats with generous tankage that generally cruise with a relatively small crew.

▶ It's easy to treat using water on board exactly as we do at home, but it's not difficult to save considerably on the quantities used.

▼ Boat galleys have progressively developed to include many of the conveniences of a household kitchen, but it's important to recognise that water is not an unlimited resource.

Catching water

This used to be a common topic of conversation among long-distance voyagers, when relatively small boats were frequently used for long passages, although the advent of watermakers and the increased affordability of larger craft means there's no longer as much need to supplement supplies with rainwater.

However, some long-distance cruisers regularly supplement onboard supplies by catching rainwater off the mainsail by hanging a bucket on the end of the boom, while a few have more elaborate methods of harvesting water from tropical showers or longer periods of rain.

First aid kits

Skippers should ensure that a suitable first aid kit and first aid manual are aboard. It's also strongly advisable that at least one crew member should have had first aid training – for boats that sail within 60 miles of a safe haven, this need only be a one-day course. However, the course should ideally be repeated every three years.

First aid kit maintenance

This does not appear on many boat owner's jobs lists, or indeed in many books, yet many items in a first aid kit have a limited lifespan and must be replaced on a regular basis. It's therefore worth checking the kit at the start of each season and replacing any item with an expiry date before the end of that year. However, this alone does not guarantee the kit will be in good shape by the end of the season.

It's therefore worth carrying two levels of first aid kits – the first a basic one with the kind of regularly used items such as aspirin or ibuprofen, Band-Aid, seasickness tablets, sterile wipes, plus a couple of dressings and so on. The second kit can then be considered as part of the boat's emergency equipment – something you know you can always depend on in a serious situation. There are a number of ready-made-up kits available for leisure boats. For day sailing a basic kit will suffice, although for long passages offshore it is advisable to carry a comprehensive kit, designed for small commercial vessels and that conforms to:

- International Convention for the Safety of Life at Sea (SOLAS)
- EC Directive 92/29
- MSN1768 (M+F) Category C
- International Life-Saving Appliance (LSA) Code

For long passages, it is important to check before departure that crew members with known ailments carry enough medication for the trip, plus their prescription. When administering medication, read the drug information leaflet and be aware of possible side effects. It is also advisable to keep a log of any medicines that are taken at sea and to seek advice from a doctor ashore before administration.

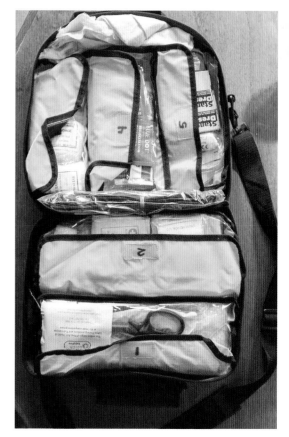

▲ A comprehensive first aid kit for offshore use.

▼ A useful day-to-day kit to deal with minor problems will ensure the main first aid kit is always properly stocked for emergency use.

First Aid Kit – BASIC

Basic kit for inshore use where medical help is easily reached:

- Triangular bandages (for bandage and sling)
- Crepe bandages
- Gauze bandages
- Elastoplast
- Band-Aid (waterproof)
- Sterile non-adhesive dressings
- Wound dressings
- Steristrip first aid pack
- Sterile cotton wool
- Scissors and tweezers (stainless steel)
- Safety pins (brass)
- Thermometer
- Disposable gloves
- Antiseptic cream
- Eye bath and solution
- Eye dressings
- Sunscreen
- Paracetamol 500mg tablets
- Painkillers
- Anti-seasickness tablets
- Antihistamine
- Diarrhoea tablets
- Senokot tablets

▼ It is always worth checking the contents of a First Aid box if chartering a boat. This one is limited to a good selection of bandages and dressings, so you would need to supplement it with a selection of medicines, as listed in the panels above.

First Aid Kit – OFFSHORE

Category C first aid kit for passages up to 60 miles offshore:

- 1 x Adhesive elastic dressing 7.5cm x 4cm
- 20 x Assorted adhesive plasters
- 2 x Medium standard dressing No 9
- 2 x Large standard dressing No 15
- 1 x Extra large standard dressing No 3
- 10 x Paraffin gauze dressings 10cm x 10cm
- 4 x Calico triangular bandage 90cm x 127cm
- 5 x Sterile gauze swabs 7.5cm
- 20 x Loperamide capsules 2mg (diarrhoea treatment)
- 60 x Hyoscine hydrobromide tablets 0.3mg (seasickness tablets)
- 65 x Paracetamol tablets 500mg
- 50 x Ibuprofen 400mg
- 1 x Glyceryl trinitrate spray (preparation to treat angina)
- 1 x Laerdal pocket mask/mouth resuscitation aid
- 1 x Cetrimide cream 50g
- 5 x Pairs disposable latex gloves large
- 1 x Burn bag
- 1 x Scissors stainless steel 5 inch
- 6 x Medium RUSTLESS safety pins
- 6 x Sutures 75mm
- 1 x Pack 10-antiseptic wipes

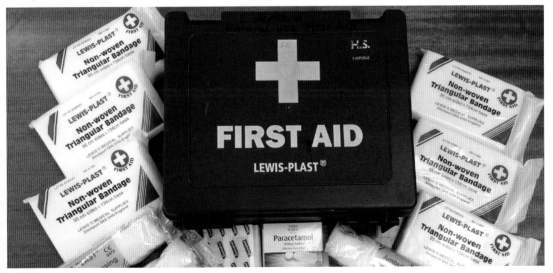

5 EMERGENCIES

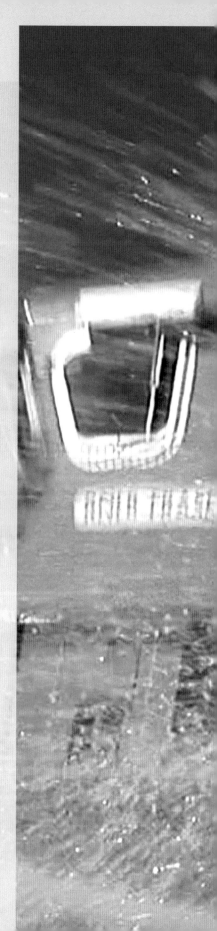

A safe skipper knows what to do when events take a turn for the worse and runs their boat without drama or panic.

Knowing what to do in an emergency situation can definitely save lives. That knowledge comes from training, preparation and experience. Through preparation and training we can learn to increase our chances of survival should things go badly wrong. Skippers can't plan for every possible eventuality, but they can plan what they are going to do if any of the more common emergency scenarios occur. But as well as being prepared and trained in the practicalities of boat handling, navigation, radio operation, first aid and more, it is their attitude and leadership skills that help skippers cope with difficult situations.

In an emergency it's crucially important for everyone on board, and especially the skipper, to be calm, collected and methodical. That is easier said than done and for the skipper there is added pressure because the crew will be looking to them for guidance and wise decision-making. A competent skipper needs to be able to decide on the best course of action to protect their crew and vessel. Unfortunately, the adrenalin rush our bodies produce makes it very easy to go into a semi-panic mode, in which we rush around doing too many things too soon, without adequate preparation and briefing.

In many emergency situations there are actions that must take place instantly and almost instinctively – shouting 'Man overboard', throwing a lifebuoy and pointing at the casualty in the water being obvious examples. But there's also a need to buy a little time to identify the best solution to a problem, brief the crew and prepare the boat. Often this is best done without the boat demanding your attention as it charges full speed towards the horizon. The old-fashioned technique of heaving to, with the headsail backed and helm down can, quite literally, be a lifesaver as often more can be achieved in 60 seconds of calm than charging along in an adrenalin-fuelled panic.

Skippers can do much to prevent accidents and emergencies happening at sea but they can't prevent them altogether and, however capable they are, there may come a time when there is no option but to call for assistance, particularly following mechanical or structural failure. Without doubt, making contact with the rescue services early on is always a wise precaution, even if there is a chance that the situation can be handled without outside help.

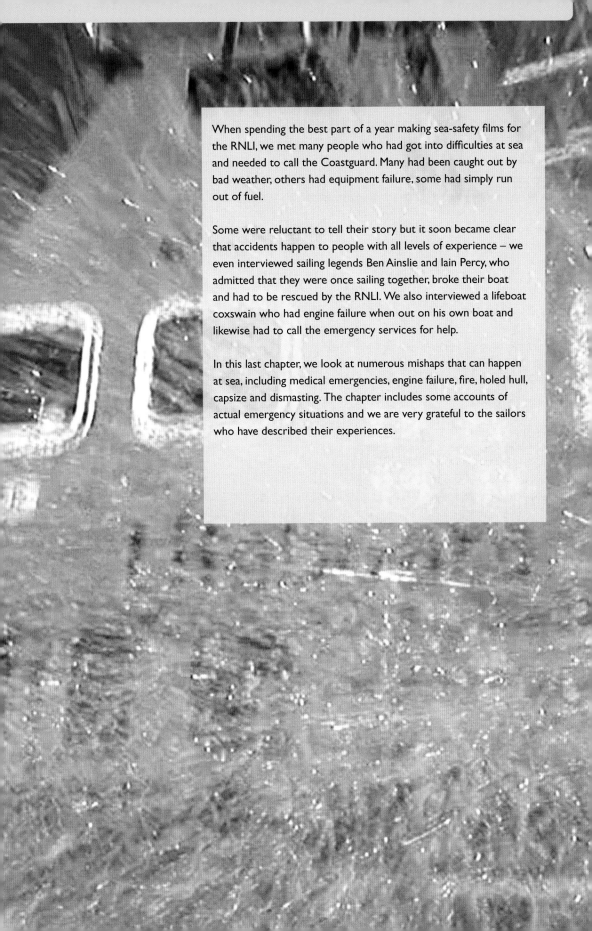

When spending the best part of a year making sea-safety films for the RNLI, we met many people who had got into difficulties at sea and needed to call the Coastguard. Many had been caught out by bad weather, others had equipment failure, some had simply run out of fuel.

Some were reluctant to tell their story but it soon became clear that accidents happen to people with all levels of experience – we even interviewed sailing legends Ben Ainslie and Iain Percy, who admitted that they were once sailing together, broke their boat and had to be rescued by the RNLI. We also interviewed a lifeboat coxswain who had engine failure when out on his own boat and likewise had to call the emergency services for help.

In this last chapter, we look at numerous mishaps that can happen at sea, including medical emergencies, engine failure, fire, holed hull, capsize and dismasting. The chapter includes some accounts of actual emergency situations and we are very grateful to the sailors who have described their experiences.

First aid at sea, including common medical emergencies

The first line of defence against a medical emergency at sea is to avoid it in the first place, which may sound obvious but should be at the forefront of a skipper's mind. Reducing the risks of accidents happening has to be a priority, as has reducing the chance of illness. This can be done in a positive, relaxed manner and it is worth reassuring your crew that medical emergencies at sea are a rarity. At the same time, there is a genuine need for the skipper to adopt a responsible attitude, which means looking out for early signs of seasickness and making sure everyone moves about the boat safely and is wearing appropriate clothing, using sunscreen, keeping hydrated and getting adequate rest.

Don't underplay the potential hazards that a yacht underway presents, things like winch-handling, the companionway steps and the boom, and ensure no one works on the engine when it is running. It is also important to be aware of

▼ Ensure the crew are aware of hazards and do not take unnecessary risks at sea. For example, working on an engine when it is running is asking for trouble.

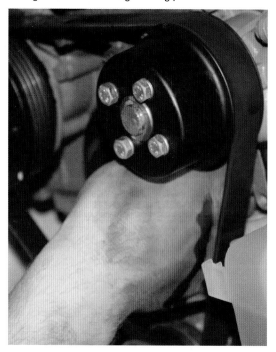

any of the crew's medical conditions and to make a note of any medication they have with them before you depart.

Knowledge and skills

At least one person on board should be trained in first aid and know how to administer the contents of the first aid kit, ensuring there are adequate supplies for the planned duration of the trip. All skippers and people who crew regularly are advised to do their basic marine first aid training ashore.

In the UK the one-day RYA First Aid At Sea Course provides basic support and a working knowledge of first aid for those sailing within 60 nautical miles from a safe haven.

▼ A 'first aid at sea' course is well worth doing for skippers and crew alike.

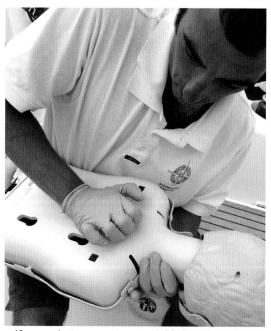

▼ If a casualty is unconscious, gently lift their chin with two fingers to open the airway.

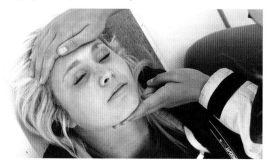

What to do in an emergency

If there is a medical emergency aboard, a swift response plus basic knowledge and first aid skills can help you get a dangerous situation under control and a potential disaster avoided. As skipper, you will need to decide which of the following courses of action to take:

▲ Look, listen and feel for breathing.

▼ A quick response to a critical situation can be life-saving. Skippers and crew should know how to perform CPR.

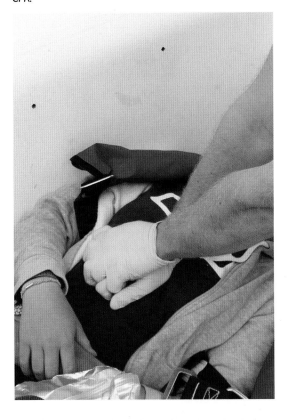

1. Does the situation call for immediate evacuation of the casualty?
2. Should you sail directly to the nearest port?
3. Should you sail to a port that is more convenient for you?
4. Should you continue with your original passage plan?

In the absence of professional medical advice on board, it is vital to know how to assess the casualty's condition and, if needs be, to administer first aid, to communicate the casualty's condition accurately to professionals ashore and to understand what can be done to alleviate and control the situation. With this information, the skipper can then decide on a course of action.

While first aid is being given to the casualty, the safety of the crew and vessel must remain paramount. Ensure the vessel is kept well under control and out of danger. If necessary, slow the vessel down and alter course to prevent the casualty being bumped about.

Assessing a casualty

Start with a Primary Survey. The Primary Survey is also referred to as the ABC check: A for Airway, B for Breathing and C for Circulation.

Airway – First check that the casualty's airway is open. If conscious, check for choking or suffocation. If unconscious, lift the chin with two fingers and gently tilt the head back to open the airway.

Breathing – Check the casualty's breathing. Look, listen and feel for breathing for 10 seconds. If the casualty is not breathing, begin CPR immediately – ie chest compressions and rescue breathing (mouth-to-mouth).

Circulation – Check for signs of external or internal bleeding. Control severe bleeding with direct or indirect pressure.

Cardiopulmonary Resuscitation (CPR)

If a casualty is unconscious and not breathing, begin CPR.

Step 1 Lay the casualty on their back and kneel beside them.

Step 2 Interlock your hands, one on top of the other, and place them on the centre of the casualty's chest, over the breastbone.

Step 3 Press down the breastbone 5–6 cm with the heel of your hand. Release the pressure, raise your hands to allow the chest to come back up. Complete 30 chest compressions at a rate of 100–120 times per minute.

Step 4 After 30 chest compressions, give two rescue breaths, checking first that the casualty's airway is open.

Step 5 Repeat the cycle until help arrives or the casualty begins to breathe normally. Count as you go to maintain pace and rhythm.

Step 6 If the casualty starts to breathe normally, put them in the recovery position.

AVPU – Levels of response

To quickly assess the level of consciousness of a casualty, use the AVPU scale as follows:

A – Alert
Are the eyes open? Is the casualty responding to questions?
V – Voice
Does the casualty respond to commands? Example: 'Open and close your eyes.'
P – Pain
Does the casualty respond to pain? Example: A pinch to an ear lobe.
U – Unresponsive
The casualty does not respond to any stimulus.

▶ *To perform chest compressions, place the heel of one hand on the casualty's breastbone, then interlock your hands, compress 5–6 cm and release.*

Recovery position

If a casualty is unconscious, place them in the recovery position. Conditions at sea may make this challenging, but ideally get the casualty below on a bunk or on the cabin sole. The recovery position will keep their airway open and prevent them from choking on their tongue or vomit.

Step 1 With the casualty on their back and their legs straight, place the arm nearest to you at right angles to their body with the elbow bent and hand facing upwards.

Step 2 Bring the other arm over the casualty's chest and hold the back of their hand against the cheek nearest to you.

Step 3 With your other hand, gently pull up their far leg from just above the knee and roll the casualty over onto their side, while still holding their hand against their cheek as in Step 2. Bend the upper leg at the hip and knee at right angles to help the casualty stay in position.

Step 4 With the casualty steady on their side, check their airway is still open and continue to monitor the casualty closely.

▼ *To perform rescue breaths, open the airway, tilt the head, lift the chin and pinch the nose shut. Then blow steadily into the casualty's mouth. Watch for chest expansion. Remove your mouth and allow chest to fall back. Then repeat.*

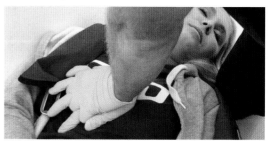

▼ To place an unconscious casualty in the recovery position, bend the upper arm and leg to prevent them rolling on their back.

▼ Place support and padding such as bunk cushions around a casualty to help maintain them in position.

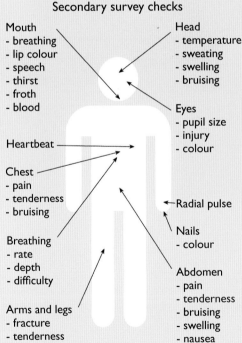

Secondary survey

The secondary survey is a head-to-toe assessment of the casualty that enables you to both examine and make notes of symptoms and history of the incident for relaying to the emergency services. Take care not to cause the casualty to panic. Try to reassure them as much as possible.

Head – look for swelling, bruising or deformities. Check forehead for temperature and sweating. Check mouth for breathing, lip colour, frothing, bleeding. Check eyes for pupil dilation.

Neck – ask the casualty to squeeze your hand. Follow the protocols for spinal injury.

Shoulders, chest and sternum – check for signs of bruising, pains, irregularity in shape. Gently squeeze the ribs. Monitor rate and depth of breathing.

Abdomen – check for pain, tenderness, nausea, bruising and swelling. Be gentle. Inspect the pelvis for signs of fracture.

Arms and legs – feel arms and legs for signs of fracture.

History – make notes of:

- Age and sex
- Time of accident
- What is patient complaining of?
- Previous injury or illness
- Any known allergies?
- AVPU responsiveness
- Medication being taken
- Any loss of consciousness?
- Any memory loss?
- Is the casualty bleeding, vomiting or has diarrhoea?
- Recent alcohol consumption or drug-taking

Secondary survey checks

Mouth
- breathing
- lip colour
- speech
- thirst
- froth
- blood

Head
- temperature
- sweating
- swelling
- bruising

Eyes
- pupil size
- injury
- colour

Heartbeat

Chest
- pain
- tenderness
- bruising

Breathing
- rate
- depth
- difficulty

Arms and legs
- fracture
- tenderness
- loss of movement

Radial pulse

Nails
- colour

Abdomen
- pain
- tenderness
- bruising
- swelling
- nausea

Also make note of:

Wounds	Conscious state
Vomiting	- memory
Diarrhoea	- dizziness
Constipation	- responsiveness
Urine	- AVPU

◄ Gather as much information about the casualty's condition as possible, by doing a full examination. Write notes and think about the advice you need from shore.

Bleeding

Minor cuts and bruises have a habit of happening frequently at sea and are easily dealt with. However, if someone suffers a deep wound, a major blood vessel may be punctured and swift action needs to be taken to prevent severe blood loss. The casualty will most likely suffer from shock and need to be treated accordingly.

Step 1 Raise the wounded limb above the level of the heart to help reduce blood loss.

Step 2 Clean the wound with antiseptic lotion.

Step 3 Place a sterile dressing pad over the wound and hold it firmly in place.

Step 4 Secure the dressing in place with a bandage. If blood seeps out, add another sterile dressing pad over the first. Add further pads, if necessary. Do not over-tighten the bandage as this could cut off the blood circulation and cause further problems.

Step 5 If bleeding is severe, treat for shock (see below) and call for medical help.

Step 6 Keep the wounded limb raised. After 10 minutes, check the circulation is OK and the bandage is not too tight.

Communications

Remember:
If you require immediate assistance, don't delay, send a MAYDAY. If you need urgent medical advice, make an all-stations PAN PAN.

Before using the radio, write down a medical checklist with as much information as possible about the casualty so you can pass on details clearly and quickly.

There is clearly a limit to what can be achieved over the radio; a better option is to be prepared and trained to be as self-reliant as possible, especially if you plan to be at sea for several days or weeks. If in doubt, do not hesitate to make contact with help ashore.

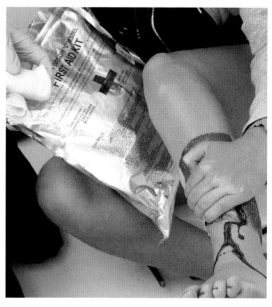

▲ Control bleeding with firm pressure and by elevating the limb before bandages are applied.

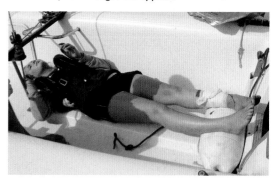

▲ Once bandaged, keep the injured limb elevated. Here, using a fender as a cushion is helping.

Internal bleeding

Internal bleeding may occur if a casualty has a fracture, crush injury, or receives a severe blow to their body. The casualty should be treated for shock and made comfortable and needs to be evacuated ashore as soon as possible.

Signs of internal bleeding:

Cold, clammy skin
Rapid, weak pulse
Shallow, rapid breathing
Thirst
Confused, restless, irritable
Dizziness
Bleeding from body openings
Abdomen may be tender and rigid
Signs of shock

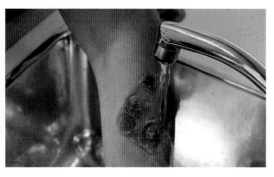

▲ If skin is blistered by a burn, medical help is essential. Immerse in cold water and don't break the blisters as this will encourage infection.

▲ Clingfilm or a sterile polythene bag makes a good temporary dressing over a burn.

▼ Splashes of fuel or chemicals to the eye should be rinsed with cold water. Cover the eye with a sterile pad.

▼ If a casualty has severe sunburn they might also suffer heatstroke. Place a wet towel over their shoulders to help cool them.

Burns

Minor burns and scalds are quite common at sea, especially for those working in a galley. These can be prevented by wearing protective clothing and footwear, but that is hardly going to be popular in hot summer temperatures.

Severe burns can cause deep tissue damage and there is a risk of shock for sufferers. Seek medical advice and be prepared to describe the area of the burn as well as the thickness of the skin affected. For the most severe cases, you may need to administer CPR.

Treatment of burns:

Step 1 Immerse burnt area in cold water for a minimum of 15 minutes.

Step 2 Gently remove loose clothing but be careful not to remove clothing that has stuck to the skin.

Step 3 Apply sterile, non-stick dressings. Cling film can be used, but do not wrap tightly.

Step 4 Elevate the limb.

Step 5 Give antibiotics, painkillers and plenty of liquid with added sugar and a little salt.

Step 6 Treat for shock (see below).

Note: Do not prick blisters, or cover facial burns or put ointments on broken skin.

Sunburn

If a crew member is suffering from severe sunburn, cool the affected skin with lukewarm water, then apply calamine, after sun lotion or aloe vera gel. Cover up with loose clothing and keep the sufferer in the shade and well hydrated.

▼ Sunburn sufferers should drink plenty of water and stay in the shade.

▲ *If someone is choking, there may be blueness of the skin and the casualty might be grasping their neck.*

Choking

If the larynx is blocked and the victim cannot breathe, give several strong blows between the shoulder blades while supporting their chest. If this fails to relieve the obstruction, try abdominal thrusts by standing behind the casualty, clasping your hands together, positioning them on the casualty's abdomen and pulling inwards and upwards four or five times. If the casualty becomes unconscious, begin CPR.

▼ *After giving 4 or 5 blows to the back, try abdominal thrusts and compress the casualty's lower chest.*

Drowning

Someone who has been recovered from the water and is unconscious should be treated for drowning as follows:

- Check for a blocked airway and signs of breathing.
- Begin CPR if there are no signs of breathing.
- When the casualty begins breathing, place them in the recovery position.
- Treat for hypothermia and shock.
- Remove wet clothes if possible and keep warm with blankets or warm clothing.

Monitor the casualty closely and when they regain consciousness be aware of the risks of secondary drowning, where the lungs are damaged after inhaling water. This can occur up to 3 days after the accident, so a casualty who has recovered from near drowning should always go to hospital for a check-up.

▼ *Recovery from drowning is possible if a casualty is given rescue breaths followed by the CPR cycle and treatment for hypothermia and shock.*

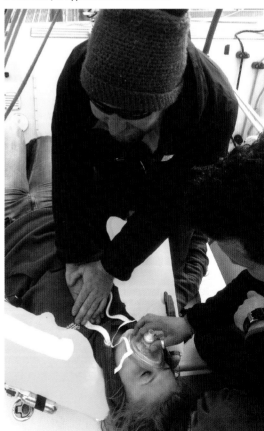

Hypothermia

Normal body temperature is 37°C. A person becomes hypothermic if their body temperature drops below 35°C. Hypothermia can occur gradually after prolonged exposure to cold, wet and windy conditions on deck, or more suddenly after immersion in the sea.

Early signs of hypothermia include: shivering, slurred speech, clumsiness, irritability and memory loss. The sufferer develops pale skin, slow breathing and a slow pulse. You should be alert for the early signs and take action to remedy the condition as soon as possible. In cold, wet weather, be aware of the effects of wind chill and make sure crew wear plenty of warm layers beneath their foul weather gear.

The next stage, severe hypothermia, is complete collapse and unconsciousness and if unchecked, the heart eventually stops.

Treatment of hypothermia:

If the casualty is breathing, put them in the recovery position, ideally below decks. Keep the casualty horizontal and commence warming. Be gentle, as a hypothermic person's internal organs are sensitive to physical shocks. Replace wet clothing with warm, dry clothing, sleeping bags or a space blanket.

You can warm the casualty by applying warm towels to their head, or by lying another crew member alongside them to share body heat. Applying hot water bottles is also recommended but keep the temperature below 46°C/115°F. Give the casualty warm, sweetened non-caffeinated drinks. Keep monitoring the casualty's temperature – if it drops below 32°C then severe hypothermia develops and you have a major emergency to deal with.

Signs of severe hypothermia are as follows:

- Casualty stops shivering
- Skin appears blue or grey, partly swollen
- Pulse is slow or weak
- Casualty loses consciousness
- Little or no breathing
- Pupils may be dilated

Treatment of severe hypothermia:

- Send MAYDAY. The casualty needs urgent hospital care.
- Handle with extreme care. The casualty is at risk from cardiac arrest.
- Check for signs of breathing. If the casualty is not breathing, commence basic life support starting with rescue breaths and then chest compressions and the CPR cycle.
- Re-warm slowly. Take care not to burn the casualty.
- Monitor pulse and breathing constantly.
- Do not rub the casualty's skin or give them alcohol.

Fatigue

Fatigue can be a major problem at sea, as people begin to make mistakes when they are tired, whether incorrectly plotting a position, slipping on deck or becoming short-tempered with others. On a long cruise, it is a good idea to agree a watch system which everyone on board keeps to.

▼ Hypothermia sufferers should be warmed using sleeping bags, dry clothing and hot sweet drinks.

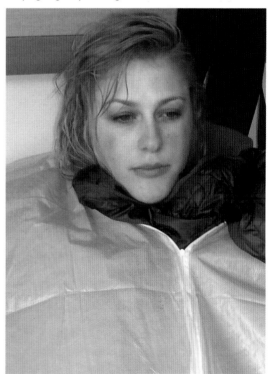

Fractures, sprains and dislocations

Moving about a boat at sea often results in a few knocks and bruises, but if a crew member has a fall or major bump and is in serious pain, they should be examined and treated accordingly. The risk of this happening can be reduced by keeping one hand holding the boat at all times and by keeping knees bent and weight low.

There are two kinds of fracture, open and closed. An open fracture is where a broken bone has punctured the skin and is visible, whereas a closed fracture remains beneath the skin. An open fracture carries a high risk of infection and the casualty will most likely suffer bleeding and shock.

Sprains, strains, dislocations and closed fractures have similar symptoms and, if in doubt, it is best to treat them all as a fracture and to immobilise the injured limb and make the casualty comfortable.

▼ *An open fracture should be supported from beneath if possible. Then gently apply a sterile dressing.*

▼ *In the absence of a proper splint, improvisation may be necessary. A plastic chart wallet is quite effective.*

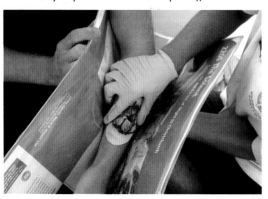

▼ *Pad the wound with dressings, bandage the splint in place and keep the injured limb elevated.*

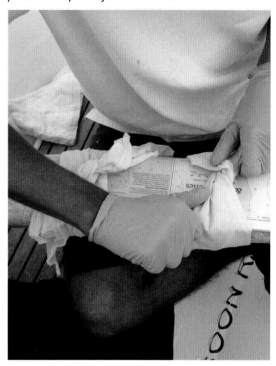

The signs and symptoms of a fracture are:

- Swelling, bruising and deformity
- Pain
- Unnatural position
- Grinding sensation
- Difficulty in moving or leaning on the limb
- Shock

Treating a fracture:

- Check for levels of response and breathing
- Control bleeding
- Cover open fractures with a sterile dressing
- Gently straighten and support the limb
- Treat with painkillers
- Splint and support the limb with bandages to minimise movement. Splint an arm or leg to an uninjured part of the body. Splint a fractured finger to an adjacent finger
- Do not over-tighten bandage; padding helps
- Apply a cold compress to closed fractures to reduce swelling
- Seek medical advice
- Monitor the casualty closely for swelling and signs of shock

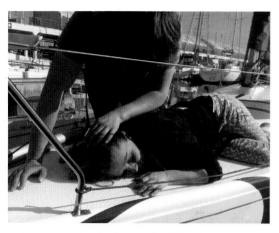

▲ A casualty with a head injury should be placed in the recovery position. Monitor breathing, pulse and level of response.

Head injury

The most common cause of head injury at sea is when a crew member gets hit by the boom. If this happens, the casualty should be examined straight away and you should send a MAYDAY immediately if the casualty has been knocked unconscious and is not responding. If the casualty quickly regains consciousness then assume they are suffering from concussion. Send out a PAN PAN and ask for medical help and the best course of action.

A blow to the head from the boom may result in a skull fracture or bleeding and might also cause a neck or spinal injury. A fractured skull is a very dangerous injury and can occur even if the patient regains consciousness. The casualty needs immediate evacuation and urgent treatment ashore.

Watch for:

- Signs of concussion, where the casualty has been briefly knocked unconscious, followed by drowsiness, headache, loss of memory, double vision and dizziness
- Depression on the scalp, bruising around the eyes, bleeding from ear or nose
- Dilated or unequal pupil size
- Irregular breathing, with slow pulse, less than 60 beats per minute
- Flushed, dry skin
- Convulsions
- Deterioration, which might be gradual over several hours

Treating a head injury:

- Check for AVPU levels of response
- Check airway is clear if the casualty is unconscious
- Send a MAYDAY and seek immediate evacuation if the casualty is unconscious
- Send a PAN PAN and seek urgent medical advice if the casualty was knocked out but has regained consciousness
- Monitor breathing, pulse, level of response and pupil sizes
- If the casualty is conscious, keep them awake but make sure they rest
- If the casualty is unconscious, place in the recovery position

▼ If a crew member has a suspected neck injury, steady the head by placing hands over their ears and keep them still.

Neck and spine injury

If a crew member has a suspected neck or spinal injury, they should be handled very gently. This might occur if they have fallen from the mast or through an open hatch.

Do not move the casualty until emergency services arrive, unless it is essential, to prevent damage to the spinal cord. Instead, immobilise the neck and head with pillows or towels and make sure the neck or spine does not twist or bend in any way.

Symptoms:

- Numbness, pins and needles
- Pain
- Weakness in arms or legs

Treating a neck or spine injury:

- Call emergency services and ask for help
- Immobilise head and neck with rolled towels
- Keep neck and back as straight as possible
- If the casualty is unconscious, you may need to roll them onto their side to allow them to breathe
- Keep them rigid and if possible have several crew members "log roll" the casualty into position, keeping the neck and back firmly supported
- Monitor closely

Seasickness

Seasickness is a common problem at sea, experienced by seasoned sailors and novices alike. Seasickness can be easily brought on by working below deck, particularly when doing chartwork and cooking. For some, quick relief can simply entail going up on deck, getting some fresh air and keeping their eyes on the horizon until the symptoms subside and the sufferer regains their sense of balance. If this doesn't work, then lying down below often helps.

To help prevent seasickness, avoid rich food and alcohol before sailing and get plenty of sleep. Keep to bland foods like bread, rice and crackers. Some crews routinely take preventive remedies before departure. If rough weather is on the way, it is a good idea to take seasickness tablets well in advance and many skippers encourage this. However, some seasickness pills can cause drowsiness and other side effects, so it is a good idea to know which remedies work best for you.

Here is a checklist of some seasickness remedies:
Scopolamine – scopolamine 'patches' are available by prescription only from a doctor. These can cause adverse side effects, so try them out before departure.

▼ To turn a casualty with a neck or spine injury onto their side, keep head, trunk and toes in a straight line and gently log-roll them over.

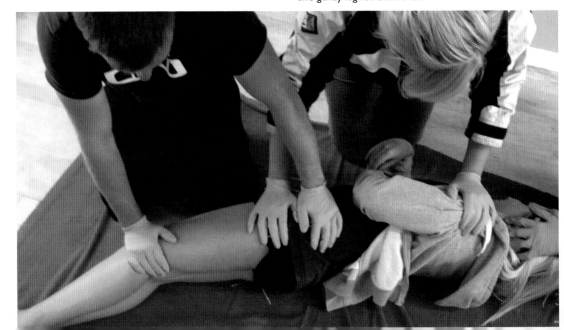

Stugeron (cinnarizine) – stugeron works well but often causes drowsiness, especially for children.

Acupressure bands – these are wrist bands that put pressure on acupuncture points on the wrist. Many people find these highly effective for all forms of motion sickness. No side effects.

Ginger – ginger settles your stomach. A slice or two of ginger in hot water is a pleasant drink. Ginger biscuits will also help. No side effects.

In acute cases, sufferers will become weaker, dehydrated and generally more debilitated. The best thing to do under these circumstances is to get them to lie down and ensure that they keep hydrated. Sometimes the only effective remedy is to get them ashore, or at least into calm waters. It is in everyone's interest aboard to watch out for others who might be suffering and help them before they get into a bad way.

▲ Symptoms of shock include pale, grey skin which will be cold and clammy.

▼ Loosen tight clothing and protect the casualty from the cold with coats and blankets. Be prepared to resuscitate.

Shock
Signs of shock:
- Rapid pulse and pale, sweaty skin
- Breathing becomes shallow
- Skin becomes grey-blue in colour
- Pulse weakens
- Casualty may gasp for air
- Thirst
- Casualty may lose consciousness

Treatment of shock:
- Lay the casualty down
- Support and elevate the legs to above the level of the heart. Loosen tight clothing
- Keep the casualty warm
- Check pulse and breathing
- Allow small sips of water only if the patient complains of thirst

Note: If the casualty is bleeding from the mouth or is unconscious, place them in the recovery position. If the casualty has suffered a chest injury, keep them sitting up.

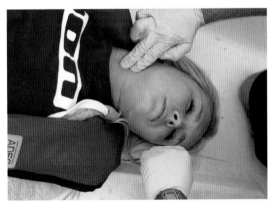

▲ A casualty with shock may have a rapid pulse and lose consciousness.

Engine failure – introduction

Providing they are regularly serviced and maintained, modern marine diesel engines tend to be very reliable. However, they are by no means infallible and around 50 per cent of lifeboat rescues are to sailing yachts with engine failure. Fortunately, a handful of easily rectified problems are responsible for a high percentage of engine failures. These can normally be fixed in a few minutes with a relatively small amount of knowledge, a few simple tools and a small number of inexpensive spares.

Many engine failures are caused by lack of maintenance, resulting in fuel filter blockages, water pump failures, overheating and other breakdowns. Indeed, one of the most common reasons for marine rescue service call-outs is for one of the most basic reasons possible – boats that have run out of fuel.

Another common situation is one in which sediment that would otherwise sit (apparently harmlessly) on the bottom of the fuel tank is shaken around in a rough sea and then sucked into the fuel system, blocking the filters. It's also possible for bacteria that will eventually clog fuel filters to form in diesel tanks, although again effective maintenance minimises the risk of this.

▼ *Always carry reserve fuel to avoid the embarrassment of running out and having to call for help.*

Engine failure – when the alarms buzz

To prevent the risk of serious damage, immediate action must be taken if an engine alarm sounds, even if the motor continues to operate. Take the engine out of gear and check which warning light is lit up, with the motor idling in neutral.

The engine should then be shut down while you attempt to fix the problem. Note that, although there are warning lights for low oil pressure, overheating and lack of battery charging, on most engines an alarm will not sound for the latter fault.

The rationale behind this is that it's not a problem that must be immediately dealt with to avoid damage to the engine, although of course it could result in the batteries running flat within a relatively short length of time.

If your engine fails or is overheating, there are a number of things to check immediately:

- Air filter blocked – check, clean or replace.
- Cooling water low – fill when engine is cold. Check for leaking hoses.
- Exhaust pipe blocked or partially blocked.
- Fuel filter – a blockage reduces power and can stop the engine. Check, clean or change the filter.
- Lack of lubrication – check engine and gearbox oil levels.
- Oil filter blocked – replace.
- Raw water inlet filter – a blockage causes overheating and can lead to engine failure. Close seacock, check and clear filter. Reopen seacock. Check object (eg plastic bag) is not obstructing seacock.
- Water pump impeller failure – cooling system fails and engine overheats. Check the rubber impeller is slightly flexible, not hard, and that all the vanes are intact. Replace if necessary.
- Worn alternator or waterpump drive belts – replace if they are frayed or shiny.

 **TIPS**

Tips to avoid engine failure:

- Keep the engine regularly maintained.
- Always do engine checks before setting out.
- Check fuel and oil levels regularly (don't rely on gauges!).
- Check drive belts for wear and tightness.
- Look out for oil and coolant leaks.
- Check fuel filter for water or dirt. Drain off any contaminants until the fuel in the clear glass bowl by the filter is clear.
- Learn how to bleed the fuel system if air gets into it.

▲ *Carrying out an engine check before departure is always a good idea and only takes a few minutes.*

▼ *Keeping the outside of the engine clean and free of dirt and oil makes it easier to quickly spot any leakages.*

Engine failure – the seamanship aspect

If the engine stops, or you have to shut it down when a warning buzzer sounds, you also need to make sure the boat remains safe. In the short term this is no problem if you're in open water with no dangers nearby. However, this is not always the case and you need to be prepared at all times for the possibility of engine failure. It's important, therefore, to recognise situations in which the boat would be immediately put in danger if the engine were to fail.

A key element of good seamanship is to always have a plan for keeping the boat safe in the event of engine failure. This will vary with each situation – even in confined waters sailboats can often hoist a sail, even if it's only to buy a little time to assess the best options by running downwind, while twin-engine craft can continue at slow speed on one engine. Otherwise, it is wise to prepare anchor and/or fenders and warps in advance for use if necessary.

The precise action you take will depend on the specific circumstances of each situation and although there are a few occasions in which an instant response is required, more often than not there is no need to be panicked into the wrong action.

Even if the wind is on the nose and there's neither enough space nor time to be able to hoist the mainsail and short tack out to sea, there's nothing to prevent you from turning round with the wind behind.

Granted, if this takes you upstream you may only have five or ten minutes before running out of water – but that may give plenty of time to restart the engine, prepare to anchor in a safe location at the edge of the channel, or hail another boat for a tow.

Advance warning

Fitting gauges for temperature and oil pressure will give more warning of an impending problem than the standard alarm buzzers. For instance, if the temperature gauge is creeping upwards a prudent skipper would not attempt to enter a narrow and busy harbour entrance with a strong tide. However, if all you have to rely on is the alarm, you may be fully committed when the buzzer sounds.

Even if the engine can't be restarted, on a sailing yacht or a twin-engine motor vessel you may well not be in a dire situation that requires immediate outside assistance. It may, for instance, be possible to sail to the entrance to a port, and then arrange for a tow for the final few hundred metres to a safe berth. A twin-screw motorboat operating on just one engine is hampered in her ability to manoeuvre, so this may also be a useful strategy.

Psychological challenges

Often, the biggest problem is not one of the yacht being placed in immediate danger but simply one of time – the worry about getting home for work the following day can add to an already stressful situation in an unhelpful way.

However, even if it's not possible to return the boat to a safe berth unaided, a little patience and lateral thinking will certainly minimise the help needed, as well as giving the satisfaction of achieving a higher degree of self-reliance.

There's no doubt that there are also other psychological factors at play – if the engine stops, both skipper and crew can easily lose confidence in the boat and in their own abilities. However, if you're in no immediate danger and can overcome the problem, it will give more confidence to conquer similar challenges in the future.

▼ *It is a wise precaution to fit temperature and oil-pressure gauges in order to detect early signs of engine failure.*

▲ A heaving line can prove very useful if your engine fails at precisely the wrong moment.

▼ Practise using your sails to come alongside or when mooring, so that coping with engine failure in a situation like this does not present a problem.

Engine failure – when the engine stops...

Fuel system problems

If the engine stops or falters, and has not overheated, there is a good chance that one of the fuel filters is blocked – or partially blocked – such that an insufficient supply of diesel is reaching the engine.

Changing the fuel filters should solve the problem and is a quick task for someone who's done it a few times before. Changing the filters introduces air into the fuel system, which has to be bled out before the engine will run. This again is an easy task – loosen the bleed screw on the top of the fine (engine-mounted) filter by one or two turns. Next, manually pump the small lever under the lift pump. Initially, air – or a mixture of air and diesel – will bubble out around the bleed screw; continue operating the lift pump until there is only neat diesel flowing, then tighten the bleed screw. The engine should now start.

Another potential reason for an engine to falter or stop is a small leak on the suction side of the lift pump, as this will allow air to be sucked into the fuel pipes. In this situation, bleeding the fuel system may suffice to get the engine working in the short term. However, this is only treating the symptom and to achieve a long-term reliable fix the leak will need to be cured.

▼ *When bleeding fuel, it is a good idea to wear protective gloves and have a drying cloth ready.*

The injector pump is a precision device that meters the exact amount of fuel to deliver to the cylinders, delivers it at an optimum time and pressurises it to a very high pressure. Problems with the pump – or with the injectors – typically result in black soot being ejected from the exhaust and are beyond the scope of being able to be fixed at sea. Fortunately, problems with these items are rare on engines that are regularly and correctly serviced.

Cooling system problems

The most common cooling system problems are a blocked filter, or a floating plastic bag that is sucked over the water intake. As well as stopping the flow of cooling water, causing the engine to overheat, the pump's flexible impeller needs water for lubrication; without this, it will disintegrate in only a couple of minutes. If the engine overheats, or the flow of cooling water from the exhaust stops, as well as needing to clear the water intake filter, the likelihood is that the impeller will need to be replaced.

Changing the impeller is generally a straightforward job. Remove the faceplate, then carefully lever the old impeller out. Replace the impeller, gasket and faceplate and check for leaks once the engine is running. On some engines, such as the popular Yanmar GM series that was manufactured from the early 1980s until around 2000, the faceplate covering the impeller faces aft and on many installations it's easier to remove the pump from the engine to gain unrestricted access to it.

▼ *Keep a check on engine belts for signs of wear and always have spares aboard.*

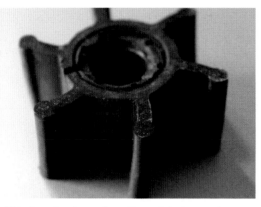

 **TIP**

Practise basic operations such as changing fuel filters, bleeding air out of the fuel system and replacing the water pump impeller on your engine so that you're familiar with the process before you need to do so at sea.

▲ *If the impeller shows signs of wear, it is time to change it before it fails and the engine overheats.*

▼ *Basic diesel engine know-how and a methodical approach will help solve most causes of engine failure.*

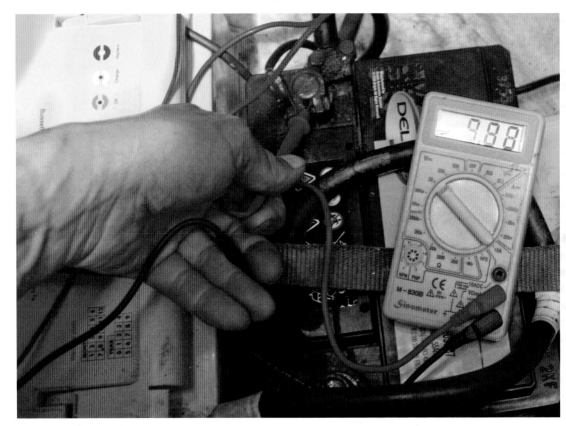

▲ *Using a multimeter to measure the voltage at the battery. It should show 12.6V or more.*

Engine failure – electrics

The motor failing to start when you turn the key is the single most common form of engine failure. Ideally, there should be a separate battery, dedicated solely to engine starting, so that you always have ample battery power for starting.

Starting problems

If the starter motor fails to turn the engine quickly, it points to a problem with the engine start battery, or the wiring between the battery and the starter motor. This can be checked with a cheap electrical multimeter. Start by measuring the voltage at the battery when no load is being drawn from it. A well-charged battery will show 12.6V or more, while 12.2V represents a 50 per cent discharged battery, and at 11.8V the battery is more than 90 per cent discharged.

If the battery passes the no-load test, the next stage is to check the voltage while cranking the engine for 5–10 seconds. Around 9V is the minimum cranking voltage needed to start a diesel engine, although for optimum reliability 10V or more is ideal. If the battery is so low on charge that the engine does not turn over quickly, don't waste the remaining charge – if the engine is equipped with decompression levers, these can be raised so that only a fraction of the power will be needed to turn the engine over. As soon as it's spinning quickly on the starter motor, drop the lever and the engine should start.

Contact problems

If the battery passes the cranking voltage test, but still fails to turn the engine quickly, power is being lost in the wiring between the battery and the starter motor. Starter motors draw a huge current from the battery, so loose, dirty or corroded contacts will limit the current that can reach the starter, with the energy that fails to reach the starter motor being lost as heat. If any terminals or connections are hot after cranking the engine for 5–10 seconds, this is a clear sign of a problem. It's possible for connections to become very hot, so don't burn yourself. If in doubt, touch the terminals with a slightly damp cloth held in a gloved hand – the cloth will hiss and steam if the contact is too hot to touch safely. After allowing them to cool, contacts should be dismantled, cleaned with fine abrasive paper and reassembled.

Maintaining the correct adjustment of the alternator/water pump drive belt is important so that the belt does not slip, which will reduce the charge the batteries receive. There ought to be around 10–12mm of movement in the belt on the longest run between pulleys. If the belt is tighter than this, then there is a risk of long-term damage to the alternator and water pump bearings. It's also important that the v-shape of the belt matches the profile of the pulleys – a mismatch in this respect will result in rapidly accelerated belt wear.

▶ *Raise decompression levers to help the starter motor crank the engine if the batteries have run low.*

▼ *Don't be tempted to over-crank the engine if it fails to start, as this will simply run down the starter battery and could make the situation worse. Instead, check through the connections between battery and starter, then other possible causes including fuel and air supply.*

TIPS

If there's not enough battery power to start the engine, check the battery voltage, then examine all terminals – it may be that the battery is well charged, but that charge can't be transmitted to the starter motor.

Emergency steering

Loss of steering is not as rare as many seafarers would like to think. However, with proper planning and forethought it need not be a major drama.

The most common reason for steering failure is a fault in the wheel steering system, resulting in the connection between wheel and rudder being broken. Many emergency tiller arrangements are clumsy to assemble and awkward to operate – some even function 'backwards', with the tiller pointing aft towards the transom. A dark night near a lee shore with half a gale blowing is not the right place to figure out how yours works – ideally, all crew members should know where the emergency tiller is stowed, how to assemble and operate it and whether any tools are required. It's also worth noting that even tiller-steering yachts are not immune from problems – the regulations that offshore racing yachts must adhere to, for instance, specify that all vessels must carry an emergency tiller, with the exception of tiller-steered boats that are normally steered by an 'unbreakable metal tiller'.

On a boat with an autopilot connected directly to the steering quadrant below deck, the pilot can often be engaged to steer the boat, giving you an immediate degree of control at the push of a button. Granted, there are conditions in which all but the best pilots may struggle to maintain course, particularly when running downwind in a big sea, when risk of a gybe is of paramount concern. However, it would be easy to set a new course on a safe broad reach, or even temporarily head up further using the pilot in order to drop the mainsail, before resuming the original downwind course.

Rudder loss

It's also important to have an alternative method of steering in the event of total rudder loss. Again, the racing regulations point to the level of preparation that's needed to ensure a satisfactory level of safety for boats venturing offshore: '... crews must be aware of alternative methods of steering the yacht in any sea condition in the event of rudder loss. At least one method must

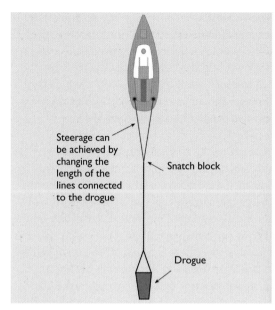

Steerage can be achieved by changing the length of the lines connected to the drogue

Snatch block

Drogue

▲ *If the rudder fails, it is possible to steer by using a drogue attached to a bridle.*

have been proven to work on board the yacht. An inspector may require that this method be demonstrated.'

While much less common, this is clearly a much bigger challenge to deal with than simply jury rigging an alternative means of moving an intact rudder after failure of a wheel steering system. A number of approaches have proved successful, but it's worth noting that a makeshift rudder is unlikely to work, or even remain in one piece, at high speeds.

However, all you need is for the jury rig to get you to a safe port at a speed of around 3 or 4 knots. Once you redefine the problem in these

▼ *A bridle is necessary to transfer the line of pull from side to side, by shortening or lengthening the lines as shown here.*

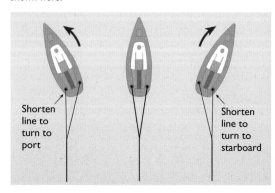

Shorten line to turn to port

Shorten line to turn to starboard

terms, it becomes an easier challenge – figuring out how to steer a slow-moving yacht in roughly the right direction is less of a challenge than steering one that's moving quickly.

Many solutions involve hanging a spinnaker pole over the transom, possibly with sheets of timber, maybe from cabin doors or locker tops, lashed to it and steering lines taken to the primary winches.

It's also important to harness the steering effects of the sails and balance the sail plan as effectively as possible.

In addition, if the boat has a tendency to continually turn in one direction, a drogue, or even a large bucket, towed off the opposite transom may be all that's needed to maintain a reasonably straight course.

Personal experience: Rupert Holmes describes his experiences of steering failure.

I have been on three yachts in which steering has failed in some form, all of them in winds of above 25 knots, writes Rupert Holmes.

The first was as a Yachtmaster Instructor, while practising man overboard manoeuvres. I was looking ahead when the failure occurred so didn't spot the problem until I looked back at the student on the helm, who was rapidly spinning the wheel to no avail, while quickly developing a very ashen expression.

To add to the interest, we were in fairly confined waters at the time, so a quick decision was needed before we ran aground on the lee shore, or haphazardly sailed across the bows of a ship in the main channel a few hundred metres to windward. Fortunately we were able to balance the sails enough to fore-reach under reasonable control towards a spot in which it was safe to anchor.

Once we had dug the components of the boat's emergency steering system out of the bottom of the cockpit locker, it quickly became clear that it had not been serviced – or even inspected – in a long time and we had no chance of making it work. A second plan was therefore needed – we strapped the spinnaker pole across the transom of the boat, leading lines through each end to a small drogue towed behind the boat. This, we discovered, gave excellent directional stability when centred and when pulled to one side of the pole allowed for modest course changes,

equivalent to turning through a circle with a radius of about half a mile.

For entering port under engine, the direction stability provided by the drogue was reassuring, while we were able to make the boat turn through sharper angles by setting a small amount of either mainsail or genoa. By waiting to enter port until the ebb tide was running, we were able to make a slow approach, stemming the tide where necessary to maintain control, and mooring alongside a pontoon was a straightforward process.

The second occasion was in a 55ft cutter-headed yawl, in the notorious Needles Channel off the western end of the Isle of Wight, again in winds of 25–30 knots. This time we had checked the operation of the emergency tiller before leaving the dock and were able to fit it within a couple of minutes. Of course, we still needed to maintain control of the boat during that time, although the yawl rig was advantageous here – with sails at each extremity of the boat, it was relatively easy to trim them to keep the boat moving in roughly the right direction for the couple of minutes it took to rig the emergency tiller.

The third occasion was on board a lightweight 24ft raceboat whose wooden tiller snapped. Fortunately, the boat was light on the helm and a makeshift lash-up, plus a bit more muscle power than expected, was all that was needed to reach a safe mooring.

Capsize

Safety is all about improving the odds. When considering the odds of a boat capsizing, its stability, the sea conditions and possible gear failure all need to be taken into account. It is important for the skipper to know the limits of their boat, how well it has been designed to cope in rough seas and that the rig and hull are in good shape. By working well within these known limitations, the chances of a capsize occurring are much reduced.

While it is important to do everything possible to reduce the chances of a boat capsizing, if the worst does happen most cruising yachts will self-right after a knockdown. Even so, a capsize can cause severe injuries to crew both below and above deck due to gear and people flying around in the nautical equivalent of a spinning washing machine. Steps can and should be taken to ensure that damage to crew and vessel is kept to a minimum in the event of a knockdown.

Stability

A boat remains upright because of the way its weight and buoyancy interact. The basic principle of buoyancy was first famously understood by Archimedes, whose law states that the upward buoyant force on a body immersed in fluid is equal and opposite to the weight of the fluid that the body displaces. The weight of the fluid displaced is known as displacement and the displaced water has an upthrust, or buoyancy, that is equal to the weight of the boat. The displaced water has a central point, or centre of buoyancy, that varies according to the shape of a boat's hull and keel.

The centre of buoyancy is not to be mistaken for the centre of gravity. The weight of a boat is distributed along its length, pushing the entire vessel downwards. All the weight acts downwards through a central point, or centre of gravity, which is similar to the fulcrum or central point of a seesaw. All the structure and the distribution of weight aboard contribute to a boat's centre of gravity.

To keep a boat stable in the water and prevent it from toppling over requires the centre of gravity to be low, which is greatly helped by having a deep, heavy keel and an engine below the waterline.

Angle of heel

If a sailing boat heels over in a strong gust of wind or is forced over by a big wave, then it will right itself once the gust or wave has passed. When a boat is upright, the force of gravity is directly opposed to the force of buoyancy. As the boat heels over, the centre of buoyancy moves outwards and acts as a lever does, pushing upwards with an increasing force. This is fine up to a point, but as the boat continues to heel, the righting lever effect reduces and eventually is lost and then the boat will capsize and float upside down. This point is known as the Angle of Vanishing Stability (AVS). Boats with a high AVS will resist becoming inverted and return to the upright position quickly in the event of a knockdown. These include narrow, heavy displacement boats with a deep draft, which can heel to 120 degrees or more. Once capsized, only a small amount of further rolling moves the hull into the positive righting area and the boat comes back upright. Boats with wide beams and shallow drafts tend to have high initial stability but may capsize at 90 degrees of heel and will not always be self-righting.

Righting moment curve

Boat manufacturers publish the righting moment curves of their yachts to show the stability characteristics of their designs. In Europe, the Recreational Craft Directive (RCD) states that pleasure yachts between 2.5m and 24m must carry builders' plates to categorise their boats in either Category A (Ocean), B (Offshore) or C (Inshore) and meet minimum standards of stability.

Rules and regulations are one thing, but the force of steep breaking waves can knock any yacht down in coastal waters, especially if it is caught beam-on. Research has shown that the most significant factor in capsize is whether a wave is breaking or not. If the wave is greater in height than the beam of the boat, then it can easily knock the boat over. Tests carried out at Southampton University in England have shown that almost any boat can be capsized by a wave equal to 55 per cent of the boat's overall length. Such waves may occur where the seabed suddenly shelves towards the coast, or where wind is blowing against tide.

This research points to the fact that yachts seeking shelter often find themselves in greater danger when approaching harbours than when coping with a storm further out to sea.

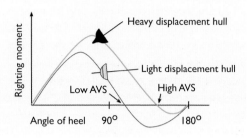

▲ Lighter, wider-shaped hulls, typical of modern designs, tend to have less stability than older, heavy displacement hulls.

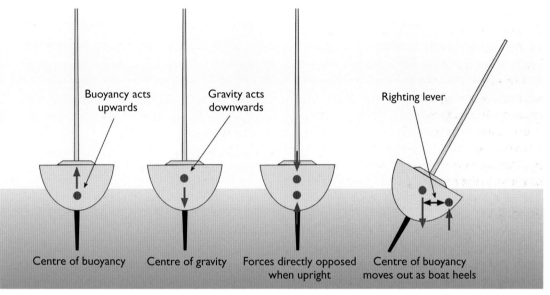

▲ As a boat heels, the centre of buoyancy moves outwards away from the centre of gravity. This results in a righting lever, or force, which pushes the boat back upright.

▼ As the boat continues to heel, it eventually reaches the angle of vanishing stability and the hull then inverts and may come to rest upside down until wave action rights it.

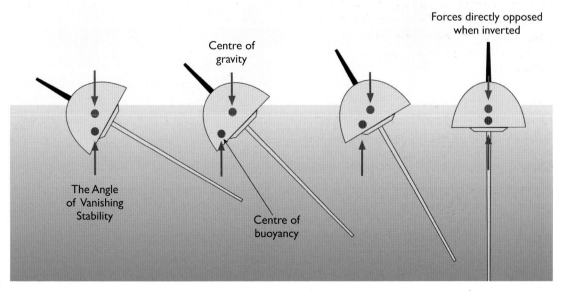

Be prepared

If you are heading offshore into rough weather, always carry an EPIRB and liferaft and make sure the crew know the safety drill. At the same time, it is wise to ensure your boat is well prepared in advance for coping with rough conditions and a potential capsize. Above decks this means, once out at sea, ensuring that all equipment is always kept securely stowed in cockpit lockers and their lids firmly closed. Also ensure anchors and chain are kept well secured in lockers as well as other potential loose deck items, such as the spinnaker pole.

All running rigging lines should be neatly coiled and held tightly in place and safety lines double-checked. Also check reefed or furled sails are always tied down securely.

Before conditions get rough, double check that all crew are wearing lifejackets and deck crew are clipped on, close the main hatch and fix washboards in place to prevent swamping below. Bilges should be kept pumped regularly in rough weather.

Do everything you can to avoid breaking waves and risking a capsize in rough weather. If needs be, heave to and ride out a storm as the boat will be more stable and comfortable.

Below decks, the cabin can become a very dangerous place as conditions become rougher. Spare some time before going to sea to check over your boat thoroughly with a potential capsize in mind – imagine it being upside down for 30 seconds and then spinning back upright. Lockers beneath berths and seats should have strong catches fitted that will withstand their contents being spun around. Cabin sole flooring, loose crockery, galley equipment, broken glass, fuel, batteries, tools and just about anything that is not fastened down can fly about and cause injury or general mayhem. Imagine also a situation where the boat remains capsized.

There will be no fresh air and it will be dark, so torches should be easily accessible and all the crew should know where they are kept.

TIPS

Avoiding capsize

- Know your boat's limitations.
- Don't overload the boat.
- Devise ways to keep things in place in the event of capsize.
- Avoid areas known for overfalls and tide rips.
- Avoid being caught beam on to breaking waves.
- Secure hatches and washboards. Close air vents.
- Pump the bilges regularly.

In the event of a capsize

- Do a headcount.
- Contact the emergency services.
- Stay with the boat.
- Have a grab bag ready.
- Try to get all crew on to the upturned hull to conserve body heat.

▼ A large wave that hits a boat beam on puts it at risk of capsize.

Personal experience:
Mark Bowden was one of 14 people rescued in 2007 after the brand-new IRC 55 *Bounder* lost her keel and capsized off St Catherine's Point in 20 knots of breeze.

Not to accept a day's sailing on a brand new 55 mini maxi would, on the face of it, be churlish! So off went 14 of us on a grey and blustery Saturday in May.

The professional crew who were going to campaign the yacht were all freshly back from around the world and were pleased to be sailing again in home waters. This was only the boat's fifth time out and perhaps the first in any sort of breeze. Sailing 5 miles south-east of the Isle of Wight with a building sea as the tide changed and in poor visibility was the trigger for the skipper to order 'life jackets on'! Ten minutes later, with the crew all sitting on the windward rail looking out over a grey cold sea, we heard a sound like a muffled loud gunshot.

At the same time the boat, already heeled to leeward, continued to roll over until the mast was in the water. As the boat rolled, all but two crew fell backwards on to the main sail and into the water. I managed to escape from under the guard wires and, as the boat continued to roll over, I scrambled up and over the hull. It was immediately obvious that the keel had been ripped out from the bottom of the boat. With some effort, I and one other crew managed to release some sheets to allow those in the water to be pulled back on to the boat and to relative safety.

People were not dressed to go swimming in the channel and quickly got cold. All the lifejackets had automatically inflated, which I'm sure saved lives that day. With everyone back on the slippery upturned hull, attention was turned to seeking assistance. Access to the cabin was impossible, the EPIRB was located in such a way that it was under the water in the cockpit area and totally inaccessible. The liferaft was also deep

underwater, strapped to the cockpit floor, which was now heaving up and down in the 2-metre swell. One of the crew who had been in the water had a mobile phone in a waterproof box in her rucksack. This was our only means of communication. With a weak phone signal, 999 was called and from then on the emergency services took over.

The helicopter from Lee-on-the-Solent arrived after some 40 minutes of searching the area. All 14 crew were lifted off two by two and returned to dry land. The yacht was recovered three days later and an investigation started to establish the cause.

Throughout this ordeal, there was no panic or confusion as to what needed to be done. While there was a complete absence of accessible safety gear equipment, the reliance on the mobile phone saved lives that day. Also the donning of lifejackets at that time was a vital decision which contributed greatly to the safe return of all the crew. We were indeed lucky that day!

▼ *Mark Bowden and* Bounder's *crew on the capsized hull. Note that Mark's lifejacket did not inflate as he avoided falling into the sea.*

Dismasting

All experienced skippers will do everything they can to avoid a mishap but at the same time will be fully prepared and know what to do in an emergency. When it comes to dismasting, it is definitely worth considering the possible causes to try to prevent it ever happening and then to look at what to do if disaster strikes.

Causes of dismasting

A well-maintained, well-built rig is not going to collapse of its own accord under normal conditions. So having regular inspections of the rig is a worthwhile expense that really shouldn't be avoided. Inspection needs to be more than a visual check, as corrosion can occur in the area enclosed by the deck.

Stainless steel can suffer from a form of corrosion called crevice corrosion, which attacks hidden parts of the structure not exposed to air, including through deck chainplates. For external chain plates, the bolts that fix them to the hull can fail.

Good seamanship will help prevent a dismasting. As well as keeping it maintained, it is important to keep the rig properly tensioned. If the shrouds are slack, then each time the boat tacks there is a great build-up of pressure against the rig and the points where it is connected to the deck. The forces are even greater during an accidental gybe, so great care should be taken to prevent this happening, especially in heavy weather.

Unfortunately, regular inspections and good seamanship will not completely cancel out the risks of dismasting. Extreme conditions or a knockdown can cause a rig to fail; sometimes rigs fail in light airs when a fitting fails or a clevis pin works lose. When the mast comes down, it will usually fall downwind and the sails will pull it over the side.

What to do

The top priority is to prevent the broken mast from damaging the hull. Until the mast is cut free from standing and running rigging, damage can easily happen as the broken end bangs against the hull like a battering ram. It is essential to carry the right equipment for your boat on board to enable the mast to be cut free as quickly as possible in the event of a dismasting. There are a number of equipment options including bolt cutters, hacksaws and clevis pin removal gear. These can be expensive pieces of kit and deciding what is best for your boat needs to be considered carefully.

Equipment options:

- Manual bolt croppers. Good for cutting wire rigging but not rod rigging. Make sure they are strong enough for your boat's rigging before buying.
- Hydraulic bolt croppers. More expensive, but quick and easy to use. Will work on rod rigging.
- Powered bolt cropper. Works like a gun, using a type of ammunition which shoots through the rod or wire. Also expensive.
- Hacksaws. A cheaper, slower and much more difficult option, increasing the risk of hull damage. Use tungsten carbide blades and carry plenty of spares. Note, cutting through rod rigging with a hacksaw is almost impossible.
- Do not rely on clevis pin removal being easy. The pins can be very difficult to remove under tension. Keep a mallet and centre punch for this purpose.
- A sharp knife will be needed to cut halyards and other lines between the mast and boat.

A fallen mast and sail in the water is incredibly heavy and the chances of recovering it aboard are almost impossible, even in calm conditions.

Working on the deck of a dismasted yacht is also very difficult as the mast and sails are no longer there to dampen the rolling movement. In some cases, it is possible to recover pieces of broken mast which can be used for making a jury rig, but this can be a very dangerous process that could easily result in crew members being injured. Likewise, saving a sail or part of it is also desirable, but the chances that a halyard will release smoothly along a broken mast so the sail can be brought back on board are again slender.

Once the mast has been cut away, there will still be lines and wires in the water that could wrap themselves around the prop, so don't start the engine until all trailing lines have either floated free or been retrieved aboard.

Jury rig

Many dismasted offshore yacht crews have proved to be very resourceful and have made jury rigs out of spinnaker poles and salvaged bits of mast and then proceeded to sail hundreds of miles back to safety, using trysails or storm jibs on their improvised rig. Mostly, these rigs will only work for downwind sailing, so having an engine with plenty of fuel aboard is clearly important.

With the rig down, long range radio communications using SSB radio will be out as an SSB antenna attaches to the backstay. Having an emergency antenna may help, but this will still need plenty of height to work. A satellite phone

will work, however, which is another reason to carry a range of backup equipment aboard when sailing offshore, to help deal with all conceivable emergencies.

 TIPS

- Plan the process in advance.
- Check your equipment will do the job by testing it ashore on pieces of wire equivalent to your rigging.
- A dismasted yacht has an unsteady motion, increasing the risk of crew falling overboard.
- Tie on fenders to cushion the hull from mast impact.

▼ *Once the mast debris and lines have been cut away and the prop is clear, in rough conditions motoring is normally the only option. Only when it calms down is constructing a jury rig feasible.*

Personal experience:
In the middle of a North Pacific hurricane, the winning skipper of The 2010 Clipper Round the World Yacht Race, Brendan Hall, went to the rescue of an injured skipper on a competing yacht.

He then skippered both boats across one of the most feared oceans in the world while also going to the aid of another competing yacht that was dismasted in the storm. His remarkable story is told in his book *Team Spirit* from which the following is a short extract.

I was so worried, I was physically sick. I've skippered a lot of boats in heavy weather, but I'd never felt like this before. The only thought in my mind was that people die in conditions like this.

The boat lurched sideways as it was struck by another massive North Pacific wave and I was thrown against the wall of the boat toilet. I caught a glimpse of myself in the small mirror and the fear was written on my face.

Come on! Be strong, Brendan. We'll get through this. You'll keep them safe. Man up. Be strong.

Outside, up on the deck of our 68ft racing yacht, the crew struggled to turn the wheel as we were struck side-on by that 50ft wave. The impact was like being T-boned by a lorry. The boat jolted sideways and lay over on its side. A 3-ton wall of white, frothing water flooded over the deck. The helmsman was thrown off balance and fell backwards towards the ocean below, brought to a jarring halt when his safety tether went taut.

The backup helmsman, who was braced when the wave struck, grabbed the wheel and forced it over as the boat struggled upright again. 'Are you ok, guys?' shouted a scared voice from the hatch. The backup helm gave the thumbs up.

It was pitch black, the hurricane-force storm was reaching its violent crescendo, the crew were frightened and we were smack in the middle of the North Pacific Ocean, thousands of miles

▲ *The 68ft* California *that was dismasted in the North Pacific hurricane, dwarfed by a massive wave.*

from the safety of land. We had already taken a pounding and the next 12 hours were going to be some of the longest of our lives.

I had to be a strong leader, keep a strong, calm face and tell the crew that we were going to be fine. That's what they needed to hear. But we weren't fine – the waves outside were enormous and every 20 minutes or so we would get smashed by one from an unusual angle, like the one that just got us. Fatalistic as it sounds, I knew that if there was a massive one out there with our name on it, it would get us, roll us over, snap our mast off and possibly drown the crew up on deck. We couldn't see it and we certainly couldn't avoid it.

I gave reassurance, I put on a calm face and I stayed strong. We were as safe as we could be in the conditions and we were prepared for the worst. But the nightmare thought remained. People die in conditions like this.

Personal experience: Graham Nelson and his crew had a narrow escape off the Scottish coast in April 2012 when his yacht's bowsprit had sprung up, leaving a substantial hole through which the yacht was taking in water fast.

Another enjoyable May weekend at the Mull Music Festival with my crew mates Jonny and Kenny.

We left the pontoons at Tobermory that Monday morning on *Java Moon*, our Fisher 37 ketch-rigged motorsailer. The sea state was moderate and the weather was clear with a north-westerly wind about force 4 to 5. We motored out to The Sound of Mull and headed towards our destination, Dunstafnish, north of Oban.

Java Moon had been experiencing engine problems; it had been cutting out after an hour or so's running. So every now and then we rested the engine and turned to sail power only – foresail and mizzen. This sail configuration was fondly referred to as The Standard Nelson by the crew, due to the family name. The wind was favourable for The Standard Nelson so the engine was switched off and we continued our journey. I was studying my newly purchased yachting magazine and enjoying breakfast. Jonny, a potato merchant, was furtively texting one of his customers about a tattie sale while drinking his third cup of tea and Kenny was at the helm while conducting a teleconference with his HQ in London (and they say men can't multi-task)!

An almighty BANG! took all of our attentions to the foresail, which was now thrashing about in the wind, and the bowsprit, which was bouncing up and down. My initial thought was that the stay from the bowsprit had sheared from the bracket located on the waterline of the bow of the boat, leaving the main forward stay for holding up the two masts unsecure. 'Right, first action – Kenny, start the engine. Jonny, you are with me, we have to roller reef the foresail.' We only managed to wind the sail in by about 15 per cent as the

slackness of the forestay jammed the roller reefing. We then tried to manhandle the sail but the ferocity of the thrashing sail seemed intent on causing us bodily harm and a possibility of being thrown overboard. Looking over the bow, it was apparent that the wire had not sheered as originally thought. Oh no, the whole bracket had been pulled through the hull, leaving a dirty big hole on the waterline!

Thinking oh ****, this is not good, my thoughts returned to the insecurely supported masts. I returned to the wheelhouse, called the Clyde Coastguard on the ship to shore radio, and informed them of our predicament while turning *Java Moon* around to head for the leeward shore in the hope of some respite from the northerly wind, which might give us a chance to attempt manhandling the foresail again.

On our way over to the sheltered side of the loch, we were aware of water in the saloon. The electric bilge pump was set into motion and Kenny was set to the manual pump too. The water level was rising at an alarming rate and our efforts were futile. I stayed in constant contact with the Coastguard, who had already dispatched the Oban RNLI and diverted two Caledonian McBrayne ferries (one heading into Oban and the other coming down from Tiree) to assist us. We were on the leeward shore but the wind was still too strong to allow us to tame the foresail. *Java Moon* was now starting to list and the water level in the saloon was rising.

As we had been leaving Tobermory earlier, Kenny had asked me what was under the cover at the side of the wheelhouse and I informed him that it was the liferaft. It was now time for Kenny to become intimate with the said item. It was the first time for any of us. Jonny read and Kenny carried out the step by step instructions while answering my incessant questions from my position in the wheelhouse about its deployment.

Once the raft was inflated, I instructed the crew to abandon ship as the listing and water intake were worsening. Secure the crew's safety – the boat at least could be replaced. We had done all that we could to save her. It was time to save ourselves.

Three men in a liferaft. None of us felt at that time or at any time during the ordeal that our lives were in danger but a cloud of sadness sat over us as we watched helplessly as *Java Moon* headed perilously towards the shore.

A twist of fate – as the RNLI told me later – a couple and their new, small motorboat, which had been berthed next to us at Tobermory, were returning to Oban when they heard of our troubles over the radio. Although the engines were new and still being run in, the owner charged at full throttle and picked us up from the liferaft a few moments before the RNLI appeared. Their unselfish act of saving us allowed the lifeboat crew to head straight to *Java Moon*, where they managed to get a line on to her and drag her away from shallow waters with only moments to spare before she was grounded.

The experienced crew boarded her, engaged water pumping gear, suppressed the foresail and dropped the mizzen. Within half an hour they had collected us from our rescue vessel and took us to Oban Harbour with *Java Moon* in tow. The tide was not right for us to be towed to Dunstafnish or Kerrer so the RNLI left us tied up to the main pier in Oban with the pumping gear. Now in the quieter waters, we were able to fashion a temporary repair. The next day *Java Moon* was towed to Kerrera and lifted out of the water for repair.

Our gratitude and thanks to the lovely couple in their motor cruiser and their selflessness for rushing to our rescue and to the RNLI and the skilled crew for saving *Java Moon*, which has now enjoyed, along with the same three crew members, two more Mull Music Festivals thanks to their valiant efforts.

Holed hull

A holed hull may be caused by impact damage due to hitting an object such as a submerged rock, a collision with another vessel, failure of a through-hull fitting or hose, or in the case of *Java Moon*, failure of the bowsprit bracket.

With immediate action, a boat that is holed below the waterline can be saved. The first thing to do is quickly assess the problem and decide whether you need to make a distress call. Much then depends on the size and nature of the hole, its location and the number of crew on board. The chances of saving the boat will improve if the crew have planned for such an emergency.

A well-prepared crew will all know where the

seacocks are so that as soon as a leak has been detected each of the seacocks can be quickly checked.

While the leak is being located and dealt with, make sure the bilge pumps are switched on and ask a member of the crew to work the manual bilge pump. If a hose has failed, in the heads for example, then the first thing to do is shut off the seacock it is attached to and this should immediately stop the leak. Problem solved and the hose can be reattached or replaced.

Through-hull fitting failure
If a through-hull fitting has failed, you will need to gain proper access to it, which may entail clearing panelling or cupboards. You may also need to use a hammer to knock the fitting out of the way and

expose the hole in order that it can be plugged with a bung. A well-prepared boat will have softwood bungs tied alongside each seacock that will fit the diameter of the fitting.

If for some reason the appropriate bung cannot be located or it does not stem the leak, there a number of other ideas to consider. You could push a towel through the hole, using a broom or boathook handle to force it into the hole. A suitably sized carrot or potato are also known to work. There are also products on the market designed to plug holes, so possibly consider purchasing these as backup.

Holed hull solutions
If the hole is above the waterline you will have a good chance of being able to make a temporary repair and keep the boat afloat long enough to reach safety.

If the hull is holed below the waterline, then you will have to act quickly. First try stuffing a pillow or soft cushion into the hole and hold it in place. Tests have shown that often this is the best short-term solution. The cushion can then be wedged into the hole using an object such as a broom handle, boathook or paddle. This will stem or may even stop the leak completely and will give you

time to think of other solutions which may be more effective.

Other options are to stuff the hole with a sailbag, with or without a sail in it, which again will depend on the size and location of the hole. I have seen this done after two keel boats collided and the holed boat made it back safely to harbour under sail, although it did take on a lot of water while doing so. You could also try wrapping a lifejacket in a towel, stuffing it into the hole and then pulling its cord to inflate it.

A sail, waterproof tarpaulin or plastic sheeting can then be used to cover the hole from outside the hull. This takes time to secure but is a tried and tested temporary solution, with water pressure helping to hold the sail or sheeting in place. Using a headsail, attach lines to the head, tack and clew. Guide the sail under the bow or stern, taking care not to twist it, and then tighten it against the hull by feeding the lines through blocks to the deck winches or, if this is not possible, by attaching them to the guardrails. The same can be done with heavy plastic sheeting or a tarpaulin.

▼ A sail can be pulled tight around the hull as a bandage to help cover up a hole, after it has been plugged from the inside.

TIPS

- Make sure the through hull fittings on your boat are easily accessible.
- Have a backup plan if your preferred solution does not work.
- Check and service your seacocks and hoses on a regular basis. Leave nothing to chance.
- Have equipment and repair materials on board that will suit the hull type of your boat.
- There are specialist products available such as collision mats and epoxy repair kits designed for repairing holes. Consider adding these to the inventory but don't expect them to be failsafe.
- Be prepared to improvise.

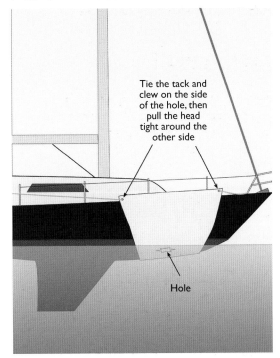

Tie the tack and clew on the side of the hole, then pull the head tight around the other side

Hole

Fire

Despite the fact that boats are surrounded by water, they are made of all kinds of flammable materials and if a fire takes hold they will invariably burn until they sink. Should a fire break out, a calm, controlled and immediate response by the crew is called for. That is not going to be easy, with adrenalin pumping around everyone's system. This is where a trained crew needs to have a clear idea of what should be done to get that fire under control.

Common causes of fire on boats

Two of the most common places on a boat where a fire can start is in the galley or in the engine compartment, both of which are in confined places. Electrical fires also occur, caused mainly by short circuits and faulty appliances. Perhaps the deadliest fires of all are those caused by leaking gas or fuel, which most likely result in an explosion.

Causes

- Smoking below decks
- Galley cookers
- Build-up of butane or propane gas in the bilges
- Faulty wiring
- Petrol/gasoline vapour in engine bay
- Flammable paints and solvents

FIRE PREVENTION TIPS

- No smoking below decks.
- Butane and propane gases are heavier than air and leaks will result in a build-up of gas in the bilges. To clear gas, open hatches, head downwind to allow fresh air into cabin areas and pump the bilges.
- Keep gas valves turned off at the bottle and cooker when not in use.
- Fit gas and smoke detectors.
- Regularly check butane and propane gas fittings and tubing for leaks.
- Keep butane and propane gas bottles in cockpit lockers that drain overboard.
- Stow all flammable liquids in well secured, upright containers in lockers that vent outboard.
- Never leave naked cooker flames and frying pans unattended.
- Always vent engine bays before starting inboard engines.
- Have the wiring checked regularly.

▼ Make fire prevention a priority and leave nothing to chance. Ensure fire extinguishers are in date and follow these fire prevention tips.

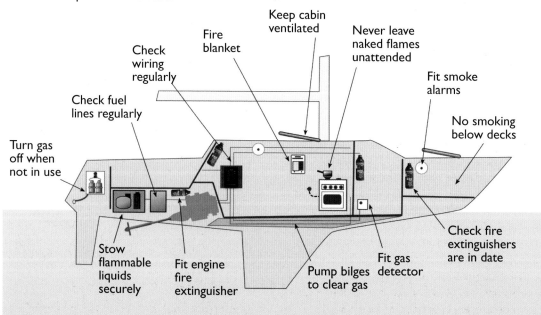

Types of fire
Class A – paper, wood, cloth and combustible solids.
Class B – flammable liquids such as petrol/gasoline, diesel, oils, paints and solvents.
Class C – gases such as butane and propane.
Class D – metals.
Class F – cooking oil and fat.

Extinguishers
There are many types of fire extinguisher. Extinguishers are given ratings (eg 13A) indicating the type and size of firefighting they are designed for. Their contents vary according to their intended uses:
Dry powder
Multi-purpose for all types of fire. Chemicals react with flames and quickly extinguish a fire. Leaves a very messy residue. Different types of powder are suited for, eg, Classes ABC, B&C or D only.
Aerosol generators
Suitable for engine bays. Sprays a fine powder and gas mixture and leaves less mess than dry powder extinguishers.
Foam
Cools and smothers flame. Best for Class A fires. Also Class F cooking oils and fat. Not as effective as dry powder.
Carbon dioxide
Best for small Class B fires. Can be used on electrical fires.
Water
For Class A only. Do not use on electrical, gas or cooking fat fires.

Fire blankets
Fire blankets should be carried on all leisure boats with cooking equipment. They are ideal for smothering galley cooker and clothing fires. The blanket should be mounted close to the cooker but not above it.

Always install, check and maintain extinguishers and blankets in line with manufacturers' recommendations. If an extinguisher's expiry date has passed, then replace it. All crew should know the location of fire extinguishers and fire blankets on board and know how to operate them.

 FIREFIGHTING TIPS

Extinguishers
- Keep the extinguisher upright.
- Test the extinguisher is working before aiming it at the fire.
- Aim the extinguisher at the base of the fire or smother with a fire blanket.
- If there is an engine fire, only open the access hatch enough to insert the extinguisher nozzle.

Firefighting
Alert all crew, and if you have enough people on board, quickly assign a firefighting crew and give the rest the following tasks to do:

- Send a MAYDAY if the fire is out of control. If the fire is put out then the distress alert can always be called off.
- Try to reduce the airflow to the fire. Ensure exit routes forward and aft are not blocked.
- Shut off fuel and gas. Move fuel and gas containers away from the fire.
- Set a sea anchor to help blow smoke and flames away from the vessel.
- Put on lifejackets.
- Prepare the liferaft in case you need to abandon ship.

Fire blankets
- Wrap the corners of the blanket around the hands to prevent burns.
- Hold between the firefighter's chest and the fire then gently lower over it.
- Leave over the smothered fire for at least 10 minutes to ensure the fire cannot start again.

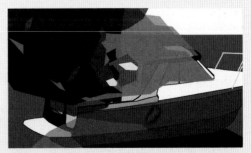
▲ If a fire begins to get out of control, do not hesitate to launch the liferaft and abandon ship.

▲ At least one member of the crew should keep pointing at the MOB.

Man overboard (MOB)

If someone falls overboard, a well trained crew will know what to do and have a greater chance of recovering the casualty safely than an untrained crew. It makes sense to talk through the MOB drill before departure and if any of your crew members are untrained, then it is important to practise the procedure. Techniques for recovery of an MOB vary for craft under sail or power, and the best method to use also depends on the size of the boat, how many crew are aboard and the conditions.

Prevention

Ensuring the crew is prepared is essential, but preventing the emergency in the first place is equally important, by wearing safety harnesses and non-slip footwear.

MOB recovery

If a crew member falls overboard, the following actions should be carried out immediately:

- Shout 'Man overboard!!' to alert the crew.
- Throw a lifebuoy and dan buoy to the MOB.
- Deploy MOB marking gear.
- Keep the MOB in sight – one crew member should point continuously at the MOB.
- Turn the boat to return to the MOB.
- Press the MOB button on the GPS.
- Send a DSC distress alert and MAYDAY.
- Prepare a throwing line.
- Prepare lifting tackle/MOB recovery equipment.
- Manoeuvre and recover the MOB.

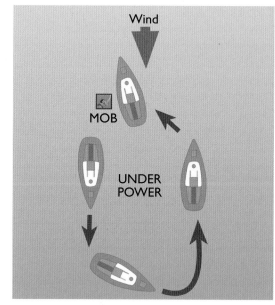

▲ Under power, give yourself enough room to make a turn and stop to windward of the MOB. Keep the prop well clear of the MOB.

MOB Recovery 1
Under power
- Keep the MOB in sight.
- Manoeuvre the boat downwind of the MOB.
- Approach the MOB into the wind.
- Pick up the MOB on the leeward side.

MOB Recovery 2
Under sail
- Throw buoyancy to the MOB.
- Mark the MOB with a dan buoy.
- If within earshot of the MOB, reassure them you are manoeuvring into recovery position.
- Steer on to a beam/broad reach and sail away.
- Sail for about 5 or 6 boat lengths.
- Tack, aiming the leeward side of the yacht at the MOB.
- Let out the headsail and mainsail sheets until the main flaps.
- Keep the angle of approach as a close reach, so the sails can be powered and de-powered under full control.
- Use one sail only in breezy conditions.
- Approach the MOB slowly. Don't be tempted to approach too quickly.
- Pick up the MOB to leeward, aft of the mast.
- In light conditions, approach the MOB to windward and drift down towards the casualty so they can be recovered on the leeward side.

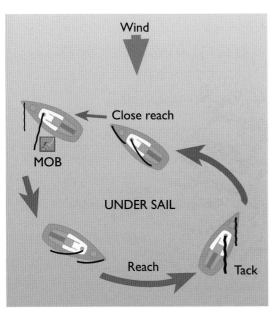

Wind

Close reach

MOB

UNDER SAIL

Reach

Tack

▲ *Under sail, steer onto a beam reach for a few boat lengths, then tack so that the leeward side of the boat is aimed at the MOB. Come to a stop by letting out the sails.*

MOB Recovery 3
Crash stop
- Keep the MOB in sight.
- Push the tiller hard to leeward.
- The boat turns head to the wind.
- If the boat tacks, leave the jib sheet cleated so the boat is hove-to.
- Push the tiller to the new leeward side to keep the boat stopped.
- The MOB should be within shouting distance.
- If the MOB is close enough, throw them a line.
- Adjust the sails and tiller to manoeuvre closer to the MOB.
- Alternatively, start the engine, lower the sails.

Getting the MOB aboard
Getting an MOB aboard a boat can be very challenging. The MOB is likely to be exhausted, shocked, cold or injured and will have little strength to help themselves aboard. Once alongside, tether the MOB to the boat using a line looped around their arms with a bowline.

Ensure the boat is stopped and the engine in neutral. An uninjured, conscious MOB may be able to be helped aboard by another crew member in calm conditions via a stern ladder or bathing platform. Consider launching the boat's tender as a first step to full recovery.

Deploy a sling and lifting tackle prepared for the purpose. Attach the tackle to the boom or main halyard and lift the casualty aboard by pulling on the pulley or via a winch block hoisting the halyard. Prepare thermal protective aids and first aid.

 **TIPS**

- It may help to remove the guardrail to bring the MOB aboard.
- There are many types of kit available designed for retrieval and recovery of an MOB including throwing strops, inflatable horseshoes, rescue slings and parbuckles.
- A 5:1 pulley and rope slung over the boom will improve the ability to recover an MOB if specialist kit is not aboard.
- Practise recovery and using the tackle before it is needed for real.

▼ *Once alongside, secure the MOB with a line and use a pre-planned means of recovery appropriate for your boat.*

Personal experience:
In April 2013, racing sailor Richard Hudson was knocked overboard during a crash gybe. It was a miracle he survived, as his account reveals.

The sailing club where I am a member has evening cruiser pursuit races on Tuesday and Thursday evenings each week. We have a staggered start according to our handicap and a common finish time at 8.30.

This particular Thursday evening we had just crossed the start line in the narrow channel near the small harbour. There were five of us in the crew. The wind was astern around 20 knots and we were on a dead run. As the asymmetrical spinnaker was being hoisted, a sudden wind shift caught the sail and in an instant we were sailing by the lee, heading for the sandbanks ahead. I could see that the helmsman was trying hard to keep our 30ft yacht from gybing or broaching. I could also see that his attempts were hampered by one of the crew in the back corner of the cockpit rolling up the furling genoa. Up till then I had been standing in the stern well clear of the boom and out of harm's way, holding on to the backstay. Thinking that I could be of some help, I remember checking the mainsail to see that it was full and well over to port and the boom was not about to suddenly gybe across. I can't remember, though, what it was I was thinking I might be able to do, but I must have stepped down into the cockpit. I don't have any memory at all of what happened next. There have been no flashbacks, no nightmares, no near-death experiences or anything of the like. But there were lots of witnesses and I have been told what did happen and know that I had an incredibly lucky and miraculous escape.

Unfortunately the boat did gybe and the boom swung across and hit me on the head, knocking me unconscious and overboard into the cold water of the Estuary. I was wearing a lifejacket but it turned out to be useless for keeping me afloat. It was the manual version and, being unconscious, I was not in any position to inflate it. Unknown to everyone, in the melee that followed somehow or other the engine gear lever got broken off in full reverse. When the skipper started the engine to

start a rescue, the result was that the sails were trying to make the boat go in one direction and the engine in the opposite.

As a result, my boat and fellow crew were in no position to rescue me – besides, they were in imminent danger of going aground on nearby rocks. Diesel engines on full throttle will not stop when the decompression lever is pulled out. Even after the fuel supply was cut, it took a while for the engine to stop and for the crew to get full control of the yacht again. We have since learned that the quickest way to stop the engine is to stuff a cloth into the air intake. In the meantime the air in my clothing was keeping me afloat although my head was submerged most of the time.

Fortunately a nearby yacht, also in the race, heard the MOB call and initiated manoeuvres to rescue me. By the time they were able to haul me out, using the hoop on my lifejacket, I had been in the water for 10–15 minutes. The sea was 5°C and I was suffering from hypothermia. Much later I learned from my rescuers that they could see I was in a bad way by then and that very soon I would have sunk. On deck, two of the crew took it in turns to apply CPR while the rest of the crew brought their yacht into the harbour where a volunteer coastguard and his wife took over before the paramedics arrived. I had stopped breathing and gone into cardiac arrest.

On looking back and reflecting on all that happened and the many people who turned out to be in the right place with the right skills at the right time, I think that a crucial factor in my survival, seemingly unharmed, was that I went into hypothermia and had expert care. In A&E they took a litre and a half of seawater out of my stomach. All the same, I was in hospital for 10 days to deal with and recover from pneumonia, which apparently is quite normal after having water in the lungs. I am back sailing and now have a lifejacket that will automatically inflate should I go overboard again.

Sending distress signals

In an emergency situation, it is a top priority to alert others of your predicament and to call for help if required. Likewise, if you receive a distress signal at sea, you must be ready to go to the help of others. What exactly is meant by 'Distress'? Distress means that a vessel or person is in grave and imminent danger and immediate assistance is needed. Under these circumstances, a MAYDAY should be sent without delay.

Note: Distress does not apply to a vessel broken down or a minor injury. Under these circumstances, call the Coastguard or broadcast an urgency call (PAN PAN) on the VHF radio.

International Regulations for the Prevention of Collisions at Sea (IRPCS) Annex IV – Distress signals:

(a) a gun or other explosive signal fired at intervals of a minute;

(b) a continuous sounding with any fog-signalling apparatus;

(c) rockets or shells, throwing red stars fired one at a time at short intervals;

(d) a signal made by radiotelegraphy or by any other signalling method consisting of the group (SOS) in the Morse Code;

(e) a signal sent by radio consisting of the spoken word 'MAYDAY';

(f) the International Code Signal of distress indicated by N.C.;

(g) a signal consisting of a square flag having above or below it a ball or anything resembling a ball;

(h) flames on the vessel (as from a burning tar barrel, oil barrel, etc);

(i) a rocket parachute flare or a hand flare showing a red light;

(j) a smoke signal giving off orange-coloured smoke;

(k) slowly and repeatedly raising and lowering arms outstretched to each side;

(l) the radiotelegraph alarm signal;

(m) the radiotelephone alarm signal;

(n) signals transmitted by emergency position-indicating radio beacons;

(o) approved signals transmitted by radiocommunication systems, including survival craft radar transponders.

Search and Rescue signals

All vessels, whatever their size, should carry cards showing international signals that are used during rescue by aircraft and shore officials.

MAYDAY distress call

If a vessel or person is in grave and imminent danger and immediate assistance is required:

Check that your VHF radio is on and high power setting is selected. Select Channel 16 (or 2182kHz for MF). Press the transmit button and say slowly and clearly:

> 'MAYDAY, MAYDAY, MAYDAY'
> 'THIS IS... '(say the name of your vessel 3 times. Say your MMSI number and call sign).
> 'MAYDAY, THIS IS...'(say name of vessel).
> 'MY POSITION IS...'(latitude and longitude, true bearing and distance from a known point, or general direction).
> 'I AM...' (say nature of distress eg SINKING, ON FIRE).
> 'I REQUIRE IMMEDIATE ASSISTANCE.'
> 'I HAVE...'(say number of persons on board PLUS any other useful information – such as sinking, flares fired, abandoning to liferaft).
> 'OVER.'

Now release transmit button and listen for reply. Keep listening to Channel 16 for instructions. If you hear nothing then repeat the distress call.

Vessels with GMDSS equipment should make a MAYDAY call by voice on Channel 16 or MF 2182kHz after sending a DSC Distress alert on VHF Channel 70 or MF 2187.5kHz.

DSC Radio Emergency Procedure

In an emergency, press the DSC radio's red button for 15 seconds and then transmit a voice message on Channel 16.

Prepare for sending/receiving subsequent distress traffic on the distress traffic frequency (2182kHz on MF, Channel 16 on VHF).

NOTE: The nature of distress can be selected from the DSC radio receiver's menu.

MAYDAY acknowledgement

In coastal waters, immediate acknowledgement should be given by Coastguard stations as follows:

> 'MAYDAY...' (name of vessel sending distress said 3 times).
> 'THIS IS...' (name of Coastguard station, said 3 times).
> 'RECEIVED MAYDAY.'

If you hear a distress message and the Coastguard has not responded, write down the details and acknowledge the vessel in distress.

MAYDAY relay

If you hear a distress message from a vessel and it has not been acknowledged, you should pass on the message as follows:

> 'MAYDAY RELAY...' (say 3 times).
> 'THIS IS...' (name of your vessel, said 3 times. FOLLOWED BY the original message).

MAYDAY radio silence

As soon as a MAYDAY call is heard, all vessels should keep radio silence until the Coastguard or other authority cancels the Distress. The Coastguard may issue the following message on the Distress frequency:

> 'SEELONCE MAYDAY...' (followed by the name of the station).

When radio silence is no longer necessary on the Distress frequency, the controlling station may relax radio silence as follows:

> 'MAYDAY ALL STATIONS, ALL STATIONS, ALL STATIONS.'
> 'THIS IS...' (name of station).
> 'The time...'
> 'The name of the vessel in distress...'
> 'PRUDONCE.'

When the Distress is over, the controlling station cancels the radio silence as follows:

> 'MAYDAY ALL STATIONS, ALL STATIONS, ALL STATIONS.'
> 'THIS IS...' (name of station).
> 'The time...'
> 'The name of the vessel in distress...'
> 'SEELONCE FEENEE.'

PAN PAN urgency call

If a vessel or person very urgently needs assistance but is not in grave and imminent danger, then the PAN PAN urgency call should be used.

Vessels with GMDSS equipment should make a PAN PAN call by voice on Channel 16 or MF 2182kHz, after sending a DSC urgency call alert on Distress alert frequencies VHF Channel 70 or MF 2187.5kHz.

Vessels with DSC/VHF radios should proceed as follows:
Check that your radio is on and high power setting is selected.
Select Channel 16 (or 2182kHz for MF).
Press the transmit button and say slowly and clearly:

> 'PAN PAN, PAN PAN, PAN PAN.'
> 'ALL STATIONS, ALL STATIONS, ALL STATIONS.'
> 'THIS IS...' (say the name of your vessel 3 times. Say your MMSI number and call sign).
> 'MY POSITION IS...' (latitude and longitude, true bearing and distance from a known point, or general direction).
> 'I AM...' (say nature of distress eg DISMASTED, BROKEN RUDDER).
> 'I REQUIRE...' (eg a tow).
> 'I HAVE...' (say number of persons on board).
> 'OVER.'

Now release transmit button and listen for reply. Keep listening to Channel 16 for instructions. If you hear nothing then repeat the PAN PAN call. NOTE: The nature of distress can be selected from the DSC radio receiver's menu.

If you hear an Urgency call from another vessel, you should follow the same radio procedure as for a MAYDAY distress call.

SECURITÉ safety call

A Securité safety call, normally transmitted by a Coast Radio Station or the Coastguard, usually contains important safety information such as navigational warnings and weather information.

The radio station announces the call on Channel 16 or MF 2182kHz and then issues instructions for listeners to change frequency, where the information will shortly be given.

A Securité call is given as follows:

'SECURITÉ, SECURITÉ, SECURITÉ.'
'THIS IS...' (Coastguard or coast radio station callsign, said 3 times).
'ALL STATIONS, ALL STATIONS, ALL STATIONS' (said 3 times, followed by instructions to change channel to listen to the message).

Note: While most Securité calls are issued by coastal stations, vessels which have an urgent message for other vessels may also make Securité calls (for example, if a vessel spots a semi-submerged container in the water, ie a danger to shipping).

 **TIPS**

- Handheld flares get very hot. Wear gloves if possible.
- Don't look directly at flares.

Distress flares

Red Handheld
Use as a line of sight distress signal by day and night.
Hold with arms outstretched.
Point downwind.
Don't look directly at a flare.
Lasts approx 1 minute.

Orange Smoke
Use as a line of sight distress signal for daytime use only.
Handheld and floating canister versions.
Lasts approx 3 minutes.

Red Parachute or Rocket
Use for long range distress signalling.
Up to 10 miles in daylight, 40 miles at night.
Height 300m if fired vertically.
In low cloud or strong winds, fire at 45 degrees downwind.
In clear weather, fire vertically.
Lasts less than 1 minute.

▼ In an emergency it is sometimes difficult to speak at normal conversation level, but take care to pause between phrases, to speak clearly and not to overload the microphone.

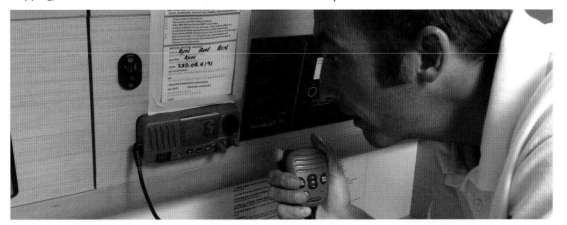

Getting a tow

Knowing how to tow and be towed is an important skill that can help prevent an awkward situation from turning nasty, especially if you are out at sea in rough weather. Towing a dinghy is easy enough, but a yacht or larger vessel presents more of a challenge. There are many variables including the size, hull shape and draft of both towed and tow boats, plus the sea state and the distance of tow.

Make sure your boat carries a long line that can be used as a tow rope should the need arise. A strong nylon rope is ideal as it can stretch and is a good shock absorber. Your best option may be an anchor line. Practise making a towing bridle, using mooring warps to make a loop at the bow, or at the stern if you are the tow boat. Use the cockpit winches if necessary to help spread the load, as deck cleats will be put under great strain when under tow.

- Plan how to secure a tow rope to your boat. The tow rope must be attached to strong deck fittings.
- As a rescue boat approaches, warn them of any debris or loose lines in the water.
- If you are being rescued by a lifeboat, follow their instructions – they are experienced in rescue techniques.
- Avoid using knots or loops that cannot be released under load.
- Protect the rope from chafing using plastic tube, rags or fenders.
- When being towed in a small boat, you will need to keep the weight well aft to keep the bow up.
- If the boat is down by the bows, you may need to be towed from astern.
- The towed boat should always steer to follow the towing boat unless the steering has been disabled.
- The use of a drogue to aid towing can be used.

▼ In a helicopter rescue, if unable to communicate, head slowly into the wind with sails lowered. It is a good idea to learn helicopter rescue procedure.

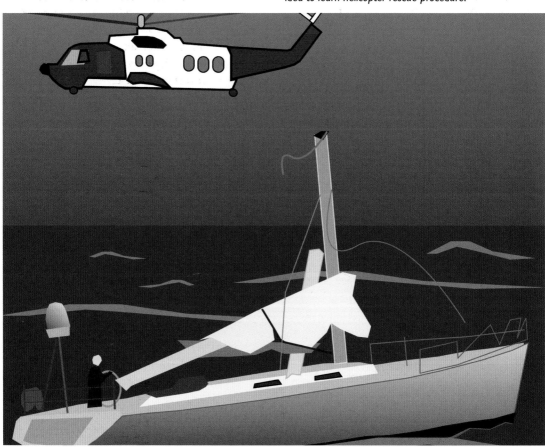

Helicopter rescue

Helicopter rescue procedure:

- Communications between rescue helicopter and vessel should be on VHF Channel 16, Channel 67 or SSB 2182kHz.
- If communication with the helicopter fails, call the Coastguard.
- The vessel in distress can identify itself to the helicopter – use orange smoke or red handheld flares.
- The helicopter will brief the distress vessel skipper before making a final approach. The skipper should follow the helicopter pilot's instructions.
- Sailing yachts should be prepared to lower sails, but only if instructed to do so.
- Listen out for course to steer, acknowledge and maintain course.
- The distress vessel should prepare a bucket on deck to gather the helicopter hi-line.
- The crew member that handles the hi-line should wear gloves.
- If a hi-line is sent down first, let it earth in the water or on deck before handling it.
- Gather in the hi-line. Do not attach it to the boat.
- The helicopter winchman will be lowered. Pull him towards the deck and watch for his hand signals.

▼ *Only abandon ship if the lives of you and your crew are in immediate danger, otherwise stay with the boat.*

Abandoning ship

If your vessel is sinking or on fire, the last resort for the skipper is to abandon ship.

Never abandon ship unless it is totally unavoidable and there is no other choice left for you. Liferafts are designed to be inflated in the water on the downwind side of the boat. They contain some emergency equipment to aid survival but this varies according to manufacture, so it is worth familiarising yourself with the contents.

In all cases, a grab bag and additional supplies are vital. If there is enough time, the crew should collect carbohydrate-rich food and water, flares, personal locator beacons, the EPIRB, handheld VHF and GPS devices, compass, charts, a torch, a knife and seasickness pills.

Launching the liferaft

- Ensure the painter is securely attached and led over the guardrail.
- Launch the liferaft to leeward unless the boat is on fire, in which case launch to windward.
- Take up the slack and give the painter a sharp tug to inflate the liferaft.
- Bring the liferaft alongside.
- The strongest and heaviest person should board first, to help steady it.
- Get all aboard plus grab bag, then cast off and paddle clear.

 **TIPS**

Before taking to the liferaft, do as follows:

- Make a MAYDAY call.
- Set off distress flares.
- Make sure all crew are dressed in warm clothing and lifejackets.
- Get the grab bag ready.
- Get extra drinking water and food.
- Take seasickness pills.

Glossary

A

Abeam At right angles to the fore-and-aft line of the boat.

Ahull A method used to weather a storm by lowering all sails and lashing the tiller to leeward.

AIS The Automatic Identification System used to identify and track shipping and to exchange data with nearby ships.

Anode Also known as sacrificial anode, a metal object normally made of zinc that is attached to the hull and protects a marine engine, or propeller, shaft and other metal components from corrosion through electrolysis.

Apparent wind The wind you feel on a boat that is a combination of the true wind and the wind derived by the boat moving through the air.

AVPU (Alert, Voice, Pain, Unresponsiveness) A system used in first aid to measure a patients responsiveness and level of consciousness.

AVS (Angle of Vanishing Stability) The angle of heel at which a boat's righting moment is zero and it will not return to upright.

B

Backing The wind backs when its direction shifts in an anticlockwise direction.

Bar An area near the mouth of a river or estuary where the water flow causes silting, resulting in a shallow patch.

Beam reach A point of sailing with the wind blowing directly towards the side of the boat.

Bear away To alter course away from the wind.

Bearing The direction, normally measured in degrees, from an observer to an object.

Beat To sail on alternate tacks towards a position that is upwind of the boat.

Boom vang (or kicking strap) A device for pulling the boom down in order to flatten the mainsail and prevent the boom from rising.

Bottle-screw A screw fitting on guardrails, shrouds and stays, used to adjust their tension.

Broach When a heavy following sea causes the boat to suddenly head towards the wind. This can result in a large angle of heel and, if not controlled, possible capsize.

Broad reach A point of sailing between running and beam reaching.

C

Catenary curve A curve in an anchor line caused by the weight of the chain hanging between the boat and the seabed, resulting in a low angle of pull on the anchor.

Centre of buoyancy Geometric centre of that part of the hull that is below the waterline.

Centre of gravity A theoretical position where the weight of the vessel appears to be centred.

Chain plate A metal fitting on each side of the hull to which the shrouds are attached.

Chart datum The level from which depth soundings and drying heights are measured, below the minimum height of low water springs.

Clevis pin A pin similar to a bolt, either threaded or unthreaded, that fastens through a U-shaped piece or clevis to form a shackle.

Close-hauled A point of sailing as close to the wind as possible.

CPR Cardiopulmonary resuscitation, an emergency procedure involving chest compressions on a patient to restore blood circulation and breathing.

Cunningham A sail control line used to adjust the tension of a sail's luff.

D

Dacron A type of polyester fibre commonly used in sailcloth.

Dan buoy A floating pole with flag that attaches to a lifebuoy to make it more visible.

Dremel A rotary tool that can be used for grinding, cutting, buffing and sanding.

Drift The distance a boat is carried by the tidal stream in a fixed period of time.

Drogue A towed object designed to reduce a boat's speed through the water in storm conditions.

Dye testing An inspection method used to locate defects such as hairline and fatigue cracks in non-porous materials.

Dyneema A very lightweight strong synthetic rope often used for halyards and backstays.

E–F

Ebb The tidal stream that occurs when the tidal height of water is falling.

Electrolytic action Corrosion that is caused by stray currents from a power source via faulty wiring, a faulty device leaking current or via a shore power connection with no galvanic isolation.

EPIRB Emergency Position Indicating Radio Beacon.

Eye splice A permanent loop or eye in the end of a rope.

Flood The tidal stream that occurs when the tidal height of water is rising.

Fractional rig A type of sailing boat rig where the forestay is attached to the mast between the spreaders and the top of the mast.

G

Genoa A large headsail that overlaps the mainsail.

GMDSS Global Maritime Distress and Safety System.

Gooseneck A universal joint fitting on a mast that secures the boom to the mast.

GRIB file GRIdded Binary data file that is used to provide weather data files via the internet.

Gybe To turn the boat so that the stern passes through the wind, permitting the sails to be set on the other side.

Guy A rope running aft connected to a spinnaker pole, used to pull the pole backwards; also a rope running forward from a boom to prevent an unexpected gybe.

H–J

Heave to To stop a boat by backing the headsail to windward and adjusting the mainsail and helm down to leeward.

Height of tide The vertical distance between the actual height of water and the level of Chart Datum.

Hydro-generator A device that uses the speed of a boat to turn a propeller that produces electricity.

Inhibitor A fuel additive used to protect against corrosion in diesel engine fuel systems.

Inverter A device that converts DC to AC current to power electrical appliances.

Isobar A line joining points of equal pressure on a meteorological chart.

Jackstay A tightly stretched wire along which something can slide. Term commonly used for the safety webbing or wire running along the deck for crew to attach their lifelines to.

K–L

Kedge anchor A light anchor, often kept in a cockpit locker, for anchoring for a short time, or to keep the stern in position.

Kicking strap See Boom vang

Knuckle A sharp curve in a frame or in the contour of a hull.

Laminate A laminate sail which has multiple layers of materials with different characteristics, which are combined to help resist stretching.

Leach The aft edge of a sail.

Lee helm Where a boat tends to turn away from the wind when under sail; it is considered a dangerous flaw of a boats design if this happens.

Leeward The opposite side of a boat to that from which the wind is blowing.

Leeway The sideways drift through the water which is the difference between the direction a vessel is pointing and the direction the vessel is actually travelling through the water, caused by the effect of the wind blowing on the side of the boat.

Lifeline A wire safety line, also known as a guardrail, that runs the full length of a boat. The term also refers to the line that connects a safety harness with strong points on deck.

Liquid penetrant inspection An inspection test using a highly fluid liquid that is applied to a surface and penetrates fissures and voids open to the surface.

Luff The front edge of a sail.

Luff up To alter course towards the direction of the wind.

M–P

Making way A boat is making way when it is moving through the water.

Masthead rig A type of sailing boat rig where the forestay is attached to the top of the mast.

Mast tang A stainless steel fitting used as an anchor plate to connect a shroud or forestay to a mast.

Mizzen The mast furthest aft in a yawl or ketch.

Multimeter An electronic measuring instrument used to measure voltage, current and resistance.

NAVTEX (Navigational Telex) delivers navigation, meteorological and safety information to shipping up to 200 nautical miles offshore.

Neap tide A tide where the tidal range is small and streams are at their weakest.

Overfall Turbulent sea caused by a sudden change in water depth. The effect increases in a strong tidal stream.

Pintle One of two or more metal fittings which are used to attach a rudder to the transom, or stern, of a boat, enabling the rudder to swing freely.

PLB Personal Locator Beacon.

Preventer A line rigged to secure the boom and prevent an accidental gybe.

R–S

Reach A point of sailing with the wind forward of the beam but not close-hauled.

Rhumb line A line that crosses each meridian of latitude at a constant angle on a Mercator chart. Not the shortest route.

Righting moment The force acting to bring a heeled yacht back upright.

SART Search And Rescue Transponder.

Scope The length of anchor cable.

Set The direction towards which the tidal stream flows.

Sea anchor A device streamed over the bow used to hold the head of the boat into wind in heavy weather, when neither sailing nor anchored.

Sheave The wheel part of a pulley block.

Shrouds The stays, usually made of wire, that support each side of a mast. Cap shrouds reach the top of the mast. Lowers reach an intermediate point, often below the spreaders.

Skin fitting A term that refers to a variety of metal or plastic components that involve through-the-hull fittings, the seacock being an example.

Slab reefing A system used to reduce sail area where the sail is partially lowered and folded along the boom in layers or slabs. Cringles (eyes) on the luff and leach of the sail form the new tack and clew, allowing the shortened sail to be controlled.

Snatch block A block that can be hinged open at the side to allow a rope to be easily inserted through it.

SOLAS V Chapter 5 of the International Convention for the Safety of Life at Sea.

Spring tide A tide where the tidal range is large and streams are at their strongest.

Stanchions Metal poles that support the guardrail lines.

Stay A wire that runs either forward or aft of the mast, to help support it.

T

Thimble A metal or plastic eye that fits inside an eye formed in a rope to prevent chafe.

Tidal range The vertical distance between the level of low water and high water.

Tidal stream The flow of water caused by the rise and fall of the tide.

Transceiver A device that combines both a transmitter and receiver in one housing.

Transducer An electrical component used in measuring instruments (depth, speed or wind) that convert signals from one form of energy to another.

Transponder A device used in search and rescue that emits a signal in response to a rescue ship's radar.

Transit When two objects are seen, one behind the other.

Trip line A light line between an anchor and the anchor buoy used to help free it from the seabed.

Trysail A small, heavy sail used to replace the mainsail in very strong winds.

U–Z

Underway A ship is underway if it is not attached to the seabed.

Vang See: Boom vang.

Veering A clockwise shift in the wind direction.

Waypoint A position along a course that marks a turning point or important point along a route, commonly used in electronic navigation.

Weather helm Where a boat tends to turn up into the wind when under sail. A little weather helm is considered by some sailors to be a good feature of a boat's design.

Yawl A two-masted yacht where the aft mast is aft of the rudder post.

Index